Practice Test for the Cognitive Abilities Test (CogAT®*) Form 7

Level 13 – (Grade 6)

Practice Test 2

A study guide to test into your school's best programs.

Mercer Publishing
PO Box 1075 Mercer Island, WA 98040

* CogAT® is a registered trademark of the Houghton Mifflin Company which was not involved in the production of, and does not endorse, this practice test.

This Book Belongs to

____

TABLE OF CONTENTS

Table of Contents

Nonverbal Section

Introduction

What is the Cognitive Abilities Test (CogAT®*) Form 7 Exam?

One of the principal tools for measuring a student's ability to enter their school's gifted program is the Cognitive Abilities Test (CogAT®*) published by Riverside Publishing. The CogAT®* exam is an ability or aptitude test which measures students on their problem solving and reasoning skills. Many of the questions on the CogAT®* exam are types your child would not have seen or done before. Most kids are at a disadvantage if they have not prepared in advance for this exam.

Riverside Publishing's CogAT®* exam is marketed as Canadian Cognitive Abilities Test (CCAT) in Canada (distributed by Nelson Education) and as the CAT in the UK (distributed by GL Assessment).

The CogAT®* exam measures learned problem solving and reasoning skills in three cognitive areas: Verbal, Quantitative and Nonverbal. Although these cognitive areas are included in an IQ test, an IQ test analyses a broader number of areas. While the CogAT®* exam measures some of the same areas, it is not an IQ test. With the focus on problem solving and reasoning, the CogAT®* exam is intended to be a predictor of potential success in school.

Unlike the exams your child is used to taking, questions on the CogAT®* exam may have more than one answer that appears to be correct. Students must use their problem solving and reasoning skills to determine the best answer, not one that could be correct. As an example, if the question was "Which one is an instrument?" and your child is given two choices: a bucket and a trumpet, the correct answer is trumpet. While a bucket could be an instrument in some circumstances (if it is made into a drum), the better answer is trumpet.

Some school districts use students' scores on the CogAT®* exam as the sole eligibility requirement for inclusion, or non-inclusion, into their school's gifted program. Others use the CogAT®* exam in combination with an achievement test, such as the Iowa Test of Basic Skills (ITBS) or the Stanford Achievement Test. Achievement tests measures knowledge in things they have learned in school (like reading and math). Typically, school districts do not use academic performance and achievement test scores without aptitude test scores for eligibility into their school's gifted program. Therefore, being a good student and getting good grades is usually not enough to get into most school's best programs.

In 2011 Riverside Publishing announced the release of Form 7 of the CogAT®* exam. The CogAT®* Form 7 Multilevel Edition exams have been modified from the previous version by replacing some of the test areas on the CogAT®* Form 6 exam with new test areas. Overall changes to the CogAT®* exam are intended to make the exam fairer to ELL (English Language Learner) students.

The CogAT®* exam is a group administered test given to a full classroom of students at a time.

What is included in this book?

This book includes the following:

- Explanations for each of the test areas and sample questions
- One full-length practice test, with the same number of questions as the CogAT®* Level 13 exam (typically given to students in sixth grade)
- Practice test answers
- Progress chart to track your child's efforts
- Steps for improving your child's scores

How does the practice test in this book correspond with the exam?

The CogAT®* Multilevel Edition Level 13 exam is usually given to students in sixth grade, and includes the following number of questions at Level 13:

Verbal

Verbal Analogies	24 questions
Sentence Completion	20 questions
Verbal Classification	20 questions

Quantitative

Number Analogies	18 questions
Number Puzzles	16 questions
Number Series	18 questions

Nonverbal

Figure Matrices	22 questions
Paper Folding	16 questions
Figure Classification	22 questions

The practice test in this book includes questions similar in content and format to the questions your child will see on the exam.

The object of the practice test is to familiarize your child with the types of questions they will face on test day, how the tests are formatted, the symbols used and the number of questions in each test area. However, since this practice test has not been standardized with Riverside Publishing and the actual CogAT®* exam, a valid CogAT®* score cannot be concluded from the results on this practice test.

How should this book be used?

The Practice Test for the Cognitive Abilities Test (CogAT®*) Form 7 - Level 13 book is designed to use for children in sixth grade preparing for the CogAT®* Form 7 Level 13 exam. The concepts and questions in this book can also be used to prepare children for other types of cognitive or reasoning tests, such as the Otis-Lennon School Ability Test (OLSAT).

We recommend that parents sit with their children when doing the practice test to ensure they understand what the questions are asking rather than letting your child get an entire section wrong and then telling them at the end. This reinforces doing the questions correctly each time they use the practice test so there will not be confusion on the day of the exam.

To answer the questions, we recommend that children use our CogAT®* Form 7 bubble test form (exclusively available on the Mercer Publishing website) to simulate the actual exam, however we have included a location to enter the answer after each question if your child is not using the bubble test form. These answer locations in our practice test workbooks are not included on the actual exam.

There are nine test areas on the CogAT®* Form 7 exam. How you approach studying for the exam depends on how much time you have before the exam - many parents are given little (if any) warning that their child will be tested and others have months to prepare.

We recommend completing the first practice test by starting at the beginning and completing the test areas in order. Depending on the amount of time you have, this could be done over the course of an evening or spread across days or weeks.

Read through the directions for each subtest and do the sample questions with your child to ensure they understand how the questions in that subtest are formatted and what the question is asking. Then begin the practice test. If your child does not answer the first questions correctly, stop the practice test and go back to the directions and sample questions. Then repeat the first questions in the practice test to ensure they understand the questions in that section.

Answers are included at the back of the practice test. Determine the number of correct answers your child had in each test area and review the progress chart at the back of this book to determine your child's percentage of correct answers.

Review the Steps for Improving Scores section for tips and suggestions on how to improve your child's scores on the practice test.

If you have purchased a second practice test, save the second practice test to have your child do right before the exam. We find that many of the smart children who are taking these exams memorize the answers to the questions in the practice test they have completed and, therefore, need a different practice test so their child will think through the questions rather than reciting the memorized answer.

What materials do we need to do the practice test?

To perform the practice test in this book, your child will need the following:

- **A parent or administrator (recommended).** Multilevel Ed. exams expect that children can read and answer the questions themselves. We recommend that parents sit with their children when doing the practice test to ensure they understand what the questions are asking.
- **The practice test included in this book.**
- **A pencil and eraser.**
  Mercer Publishing's CogAT®* Form 7 bubble test form (recommended). Exams are often scored electronically using bubble test forms. Many children have never seen a bubble test form prior to exam day and errors can be made from using the form incorrectly. Children can mark the correct answer in the wrong bubble and circles that are incorrectly filled in or answer sheets that contain stray marks may negatively impact your child's score on the exam. While it is not required, we highly recommended your child use our bubble test form when they do our practice test to simulate the exam. Our CogAT Form 7 bubble test forms are exclusively available on the Mercer Publishing website.

What else can we do to improve my child's score?

Once your child takes our practice test, there are several proactive steps that you can take that may increase your child's score. We have included a progress chart and a Steps for Improving Scores section devoted to this topic.

Mercer Publishing has a full set of materials in The Gifted Program® Series to help your child score as well as they can on their gifted program entrance exam.

For more on available materials, visit our website at www.mercerpublishing.com.

Now, on to the practice test.

Practice Test 2

Verbal Analogies

Directions

In the Verbal Analogies subtest, students are given a pair of words and another word without its pair. The first pair of words is related in some way. Students must determine how they are related and then select the word from the available answers that has the same relationship with the third word.

Sample Questions

1.

big → biggest : small →

A. tiny   B. smallest   C. elfin   D. weak   E. young

In this analogy, the first pair is big and biggest – biggest is form of big used when comparing three or more items. In the second pair, you are given small and must select the word that has the same relationship as the first pair. The form of small you would use when comparing three or more items is...

The correct answer is B. smallest. B is the answer you would mark on the bubble test form or in the available answer field*.

2.

finger → hand : toe →

A. foot   B. polish   C. toenail   D. leg   E. ankle

In this analogy, the first pair is finger and hand – a finger is part of a hand. In the second pair, you are given toe and must select the word that has the same relationship as the first pair. Toe is part of a...

The correct answer is A. foot. A is the answer you would mark on the bubble test form or in the available answer field*.

* Answer fields will not be in your child's exam workbook. Bubble test forms are typically used during the exam and marking your answers on a bubble test form as they do the practice test is recommended.

Begin

1. rose → flower : oak →

A. plant B. acorn C. book D. tree E. pine

Answer: __________

2. brush → paint : hose →

A. fire B. water C. garden D. rubber E. vegetable

Answer: __________

3. fins → fish : wings →

A. feathers B. flight C. antennae D. airplane E. arm

Answer: __________

4. bee → hive : bat →

A. wings B. ball C. team D. baseball E. cave

Answer: __________

Continue

5. dish → cabinet : book →

A. teacher B. shelf C. paragraph D. bookstore E. nonfiction

Answer: __________

6. nostril → nose : spout →

A. elephant B. pitcher C. bowl D. seed E. water

Answer: __________

7. dude → boy : buck →

A. deer B. kick C. girl D. dollar E. help

Answer: __________

8. page → book : website →

A. designer B. search C. click D. desktop E. internet

Answer: __________

Continue

9. almond → nut : pork →

A. beef B. bacon C. meat D. pig E. breakfast

Answer: __________

10. hide → seek : cops →

A. robbers B. police C. investigate D. arrest E. crime

Answer: __________

11. jewel → crown : pepperoni →

A. refrigerator B. pizza C. pepper D. meat E. sausage

Answer: __________

12. deck → card : skeleton →

A. ghost B. body C. bone D. skin E. person

Answer: __________

Continue

13. greed → money : hunger →

A. thirst B. food C. starve D. fork E. appetite

Answer: _________

14. sister → sibling : daughter →

A. mother B. girl C. son D. brother E. child

Answer: _________

15. Wednesday → Tuesday : Tuesday →

A. Wednesday B. Monday C. Friday D. Tuesday E. Saturday

Answer: _________

16. carton → milk : pen →

A. pencil B. paper C. ink D. backpack E. desk

Answer: _________

Continue

17. insignificant → trickle : major →

A. magic B. drip C. precipitation D. flood E. need

Answer: __________

18. limb → tree : speaker →

A. podium B. radio C. speech D. oral E. conference

Answer: __________

19. tire → rubber : box →

A. mail B. lid C. container D. cardboard E. bed

Answer: __________

20. sour → taste : novel →

A. mystery B. assignment C. book D. magazine E. reading

Answer: __________

Continue

21. drawer → pull : door →

A. gate B. doorbell C. window D. house E. knob

Answer: __________

22. solitary → one : multitudes →

A. two B. single C. many D. equation E. addition

Answer: __________

23. massage → spa : boxing →

A. glove B. ring C. jogging D. sport E. jab

Answer: __________

24. author → books : poet →

A. novels B. writers C. words D. poems E. romance

Answer: __________

STOP!

Sentence Completion

Directions

In the Sentence Completion subtest, students are given a sentence that is missing a word. Students must determine which of the available answers best completes the sentence.

Sample Questions

1.

The dog _______________ at the delivery man.

A. mooed B. meowed C. yelled D. frowned E. barked

The correct answer is E. barked. E is the answer you would mark on the bubble test form or in the available answer field*.

2.

Ice cream _______________ if it doesn't stay cold.

A. tires B. melts C. licks D. freezes E. enjoys

The correct answer is B. melts. B is the answer you would mark on the bubble test form or in the available answer field*.

* Answer fields will not be in your child's exam workbook. Bubble test forms are typically used during the exam and marking your answers on a bubble test form as they do the practice test is recommended.

Begin

1. Luckily, no one was _______________ in the accident.

A. mistaken B. late C. hurt D. insured E. hit

Answer: _________

2. Jonah could not _______________ why his dog kept barking all night.

A. understand B. care C. forget D. limit E. propose

Answer: _________

3. Kate was sent into the conference room to _______________ the final points of the multi-million dollar contract.

A. start B. collect C. spend D. terminate E. negotiate

Answer: _________

4. After spending the money that he owed his parents, Alexander found himself in a(n) _______________.

A. field B. predicament C. jail D. racecar E. punishment

Answer: _________

Continue

5. After a few minutes, your eyes become _______________ in a dark room.

A. closed B. adjusted C. wider D. different E. darker

Answer: _________

6. Sara's behavior ______________the teachers on the field trip because she was usually so well behaved in class.

A. inspired B. understood C. taught D. surprised E. obeyed

Answer: _________

7. In many states it is _______________ for motorcyclists not to wear a helmet.

A. required B. damaging C. unwise D. illegal E. difficult

Answer: _________

8. No one could explain why Burt _______________ Lucy's bike even though he had one of his own.

A. sketched B. broke C. stole D. sold E. repaired

Answer: _________

Continue

9. When they found out the _______________ in the hotel was broken, they took the stairs.

A. room B. phone C. car D. handrail E. elevator

Answer: _________

10. The students were extremely _______________, but most of them couldn't arrive to class on time.

A. late B. intelligent C. relaxed D. important E. hungry

Answer: _________

11. Peggy smiled from ear to ear because she never _______________ that things would turn out so well.

A. decided B. measured C. calculated D. required E. thought

Answer: _________

12. It may seem harsh to punish him, but he has to learn that what he did is _______________.

A. exhausting B. over C. unacceptable D. necessary E. minor

Answer: _________

Continue

13. To be wise is to apply _______________ to real-life situations

A. equations B. contracts C. stories D. knowledge E. little

Answer: _________

14. Even though visually they look like they converge on the horizon, the two rails of a railroad track are actually ______________to each other.

A. diverging B. parallel C. useful D. tied E. unrelated

Answer: _________

15. Even though a _______________ is a fruit, you shouldn't put it in a fruit salad.

A. fruit B. tomato C. peach D. carrot E. banana

Answer: _________

16. The _______________ had a floral pattern of roses in bright colors.

A. garden B. newspaper C. tulips D. tablecloth E. hose

Answer: _________

Continue

17. I should have added rather than subtracted. That makes ______________.

A. math B. shivers C. sense D. questions E. up

Answer: __________

18. I would have waited for you if you told me you would ______________.

A. know B. wait C. leave D. believe E. come

Answer: __________

19. Beggars sometimes sell relatively ______________ items in order to circumvent laws against panhandling.

A. expensive B. heavy C. stolen D. worthless E. old

Answer: __________

20. Susan was not sure how long the dress was, so she gave the tailor a(n) ______________ measurement.

A. exact B. rushed C. personal D. length E. approximate

Answer: __________

STOP!

Verbal Classification

Directions

In the Verbal Classification subtest, each question has two rows of words. In the top row, the student is given a set of three words that are similar in some way. Students must determine how they are similar and then select the word from the available answers that is most similar to the words on the top row.

Sample Questions

1. yellow purple green

A. caterpillar B. brown C. chalk D. pretty E. colorful

The correct answer is B. brown. B is the answer you would mark on the bubble test form or in the available answer field*.

2. triangle diamond oval

A. ball B. circle C. shape D. baseball E. character

The correct answer is B. circle. B is the answer you would mark on the bubble test form or in the available answer field*.

* Answer fields will not be in your child's exam workbook. Bubble test forms are typically used during the exam and marking your answers on a bubble test form as they do the practice test is recommended.

Begin

1. throw bat slide

A. pitch B. dribble C. rebound D. baseball E. serve

Answer: __________

2. mow trim clip

A. grab B. climb C. weld D. swim E. rake

Answer: __________

3. Saturn Mars Jupiter

A. planets B. sun C. space D. orbit E. Earth

Answer: __________

4. angel-food chocolate birthday

A. chicken B. gift C. red velvet D. baking E. balloons

Answer: __________

Continue

5. oak maple cedar

A. lumber B. wood C. hickory D. hammer E. fence

Answer: _________

6. horse motorcycle train

A. shoes B. station C. dog D. chair E. skateboard

Answer: _________

7. German Chinese Italian

A. USA B. Mexico C. Colosseum D. Canada E. Spanish

Answer: _________

8. foot basket soccer

A. ball B. sport C. team D. volley E. coach

Answer: _________

Continue

9. skunk zebra Dalmatian

A. dice B. crow C. kitten D. panda E. robin

Answer: __________

10. pound quart gram

A. size B. ounce C. liquid D. dollar E. container

Answer: __________

11. harmonica trumpet flute

A. piano B. guitar C. harp D. drum E. whistle

Answer: __________

12. diversity assortment mixture

A. variety B. group C. criteria D. characteristic E. alliance

Answer: __________

Continue

13. galaxy star planet

A. moon B. astronomy C. space D. astronaut E. rocket

Answer: _________

14. liver bladder heart

A. belt B. kidney C. tongue D. muscle E. skeleton

Answer: _________

15. architect plumber electrician

A. actor B. toaster C. carpenter D. elevator E. building

Answer: _________

16. elude escape avoid

A. capture B. flee C. stand D. free E. prison

Answer: _________

Continue

17. hall den garage

A. bath B. school C. resident D. neighborhood E. bathroom

Answer: __________

18. car toolset ladder

A. toilet B. guitar C. bicycle D. sofa E. oven

Answer: __________

19. dew fog rain

A. mist B. snow C. hail D. humility E. hurricane

Answer: __________

20. sadness depression sorrow

A. elation B. ambivalence C. distress D. optimism E. hurried

Answer: __________

STOP!

Number Analogies

Directions

In the Number Analogies subtest, students are given two pairs of numbers and another number without its pair. The first two pairs of numbers are related in some way. Students must determine how they are related and then select the number from the available answers that has the same relationship with the number in the third pair.

Sample Questions

1. [2 → 2] [4 → 4] [6 → ?]

A. 3 B. 4 C. 5 D. 6 E. 7

The correct answer is D. 6. D is the answer you would mark on the bubble test form or in the available answer field*.

2. [2 → 1] [5 → 4] [8 → ?]

A. 4 B. 5 C. 6 D. 7 E. 8

The correct answer is D. 7. D is the answer you would mark on the bubble test form or in the available answer field*.

* Answer fields will not be in your child's exam workbook. Bubble test forms are typically used during the exam and marking your answers on a bubble test form as they do the practice test is recommended.

Begin →

1. [4 → 12] [1 → 3] [7 → ?]

A. 18 B. 19 C. 20 D. 21 E. 22

Answer: __________

2. [14 → 1] [22 → 9] [19 → ?]

A. 3 B. 6 C. 9 D. 12 E. 15

Answer: __________

3. [0 → 1] [8 → 25] [5 → ?]

A. 12 B. 14 C. 16 D. 18 E. 20

Answer: __________

4. [14 → 7] [24 → 12] [28 → ?]

A. 17 B. 8 C. 11 D. 12 E. 14

Answer: __________

Continue

5. [50 → 10] [15 → 3] [110→ ?]

A. 14 B. 16 C. 18 D. 20 E. 22

Answer: __________

6. [9→ 3] [21 → 7] [15 → ?]

A. 3 B. 4 C. 5 D. 6 E. 7

Answer: __________

7. [2 → 6] [3 → 9] [7 → ?]

A. 16 B. 18 C. 20 D. 21 E. 22

Answer: __________

8. [2 → 9] [10 → 17] [5 → ?]

A. 10 B. 11 C. 12 D. 13 E. 1 4

Answer: __________

Continue

9. [10 → 18] [5 → 8] [9 → ?]

A. 16 B. 20 C. 24 D. 28 E. 32

Answer: __________

10. [9 → 22] [3 → 16] [7→ ?]

A. 19 B. 20 C. 21 D. 22 E. 23

Answer: __________

11. [16 → 7] [10 → 4] [12→ ?]

A. 1 B. 2 C. 3 D. 5 E. 8

Answer: __________

12. [15→ 7] [18 → 10] [12 → ?]

A. 0 B. 1 C. 2 D. 3 E. 4

Answer: __________

Continue

13. [6 → 22] [8 → 28] [11 → ?]

A. 35 B. 36 C. 37 D. 38 E. 39

Answer: _________

14. [18 → 6] [17 → 5] [21 → ?]

A. 8 B. 9 C. 10 D. 11 E. 12

Answer: _________

15. [6 → 7] [5→ 5] [8 → ?]

A. 2 B. 5 C. 8 D. 11 E. 14

Answer: _________

16. [0 → 1] [18→ 7] [9 → ?]

A. 2 B. 3 C. 4 D. 6 E. 8

Answer: _________

Continue

17. [6 → 25] [0→ 1] [8 → ?]

A. 30 B. 31 C. 32 D. 33 E. 34

Answer: __________

18. [3 → 7] [4 → 10] [6 → ?]

A. 15 B. 16 C. 17 D. 18 E. 19

Answer: __________

Number Puzzles

Directions

In the Number Puzzles subtest, students are given a mathematical equation and students must determine the number from the available answers that should replace the question mark in the equation.

Sample Questions

There are two types of questions that may be found in the number puzzles subtest:

1. (2 + 2) + 2 = (2 + ?) + 2

A. 2 B. 4 C. 6 D. 8 E. 10

The correct answer is A. 2. A is the answer you would mark on the bubble test form or in the available answer field*.

2. 4 + ■ = ?

■ = 2

A. 2 B. 4 C. 6 D. 8 E. 10

In this number puzzles problem, the student must substitute the value for ■ (2) in the equation to determine the value for the question mark. The correct answer is C. 6. C is the answer you would mark on the bubble test form or in the available answer field*.

* Answer fields will not be in your child's exam workbook. Bubble test forms are typically used during the exam and marking your answers on a bubble test form as they do the practice test is recommended.

Begin

1. ? ÷ 7 = 8

A. 48 B. 50 C. 52 D. 54 E. 56

Answer: __________

2. 33 x ? = 90 + 9

A. 1 B. 2 C. 3 D. 4 E. 5

Answer: __________

3. ◊ x 7 = ?

◊ = 8

A. 64 B. 60 C. 56 D. 52 E. 48

Answer: __________

4. ● + ● + 4 - ◆ = 3 + ?

● = 7
◆ = 9

A. 6 B. 7 C. 8 D. 9 E. 10

Answer: __________

Continue

5. ● + □ = ?

● = □ + □
□ = 3

A. 7 B. 9 C. 11 D. 12 E. 13

Answer: __________

6. (● ÷ ◊) + 5 = ?

● = 36
◊ = 4

A. 11 B. 12 C. 13 D. 14 E. 15

Answer: __________

7. (◊ - 4) ÷ ● = ?

◊ = 25
● = 3 + 4

A. 1 B. 2 C. 3 D. 4 E. 5

Answer: __________

8. ◆ + ● - ○ = ?

◆ = 2
● = ◆ x ◆
○ = 3

A. 1 B. 2 C. 3 D. 4 E. 5

Answer: __________

Continue

9. ◆ - 3 = 35 ÷ ?

◆ = 8

A. 7 B. 6 C. 5 D. 4 E. 3

Answer: __________

10. ♢ x ○ = ?

♢ = 6 - 2
○ = 5 + ♢

A. 28 B. 36 C. 49 D. 54 E. 63

Answer: __________

11. (■ - ○) x ? = ◆

■ = 14 - 4
○ = 8
◆ = 8

A. 4 B. 5 C. 6 D. 7 E. 8

Answer: __________

12. (◆ x ○) + ○ - ◆ = ?

◆ = 7 - 1
○ = 4

A. 23 B. 22 C. 21 D. 20 E. 19

Answer: __________

Continue

13. ? ÷ 3 = □ x 2

□ = 5

A. 15 B. 21 C. 30 D. 33 E. 36

Answer: __________

14. (▲ x 3) - ◇ = ?

▲ = 3
◇ = ▲ x ▲

A. 0 B. 1 C. 2 D. 3 E. 4

Answer: __________

15. ▲ + ◇ + ● = ?

▲ = 3
◇ = ● + ▲
● = ▲ + ▲

A. 15 B. 16 C. 17 D. 18 E. 19

Answer: __________

16. ○ + ? = ● + ◆ + ◆

○ = ● + 2
◆ = ● + 3
● = 3 + 2

A. 13 B. 14 C. 15 D. 16 E. 17

Answer: __________

STOP!

Number Series

Directions

In the Number Series subtest, the student is shown a series of numbers. Students need to review the numbers to determine the rule or pattern used and then select the number from the answer choices that should come next in the series.

Sample Questions

1. 1 2 3 4 5 →

A. 4 B. 5 C. 6 D. 7 E. 8

The correct answer is C. 6. C is the answer you would mark on the bubble test form or in the available answer field*.

2. 0 5 0 5 0 →

A. 5 B. 7 C. 0 D. 3 E. 6

The correct answer is A. 5. A is the answer you would mark on the bubble test form or in the available answer field*.

* Answer fields will not be in your child's exam workbook. Bubble test forms are typically used during the exam and marking your answers on a bubble test form as they do the practice test is recommended.

Begin

1. 2 5 4 7 6 →

A. 7 B. 8 C. 9 D. 10 E. 11

Answer: __________

2. 31 27 29 25 27 →

A. 23 B. 24 C. 25 D. 26 E. 27

Answer: __________

3. 16 11 7 4 2 →

A. 4 B. 3 C. 2 D. 1 E. 0

Answer: __________

4. 7 8 10 11 13 14 16 →

A. 14 B. 15 C. 16 D. 17 E. 18

Answer: __________

Continue

5. 5 6 8 11 15 →

A. 9 B. 13 C. 20 D. 22 E. 24

Answer: __________

6. 7 40 10 35 13 31 16 →

A. 20 B. 18 C. 30 D. 29 E. 28

Answer: __________

7. 9 7 10 8 →

A. 9 B. 11 C. 13 D. 15 E. 17

Answer: __________

8. 57 58 60 63 68 →

A. 75 B. 76 C. 80 D. 82 E. 84

Answer: __________

Continue

9. 4 8 13 19 26 →

A. 30 B. 41 C. 32 D. 33 E. 34

Answer: __________

10. 14 7 9 9 7 →

A. 9 B. 14 C. 12 D. 10 E. 7

Answer: __________

11. 53 29 17 11 →

A. 5 B. 6 C. 7 D. 8 E. 9

Answer: __________

12. 256 64 32 8 →

A. 0 B. 1 C. 2 D. 3 E. 4

Answer: __________

Continue

13. 4 16 3 9 2 4 →

A. 0 B. 1 C. 3 D. 7 E. 11

Answer: _________

14. 7 9 9 5 7 7 →

A. 3 B. 4 C. 5 D. 6 E. 7

Answer: _________

15. 2 7 4 8 13 10 14 →

A. 11 B. 13 C. 15 D. 17 E. 19

Answer: _________

16. 7 14 21 4 8 →

A. 6 B. 8 C. 10 D. 12 E. 14

Answer: _________

Continue

17. 27 54 18 36 12 24 →

A. 2 B. 4 C. 8 D. 12 E. 32

Answer: __________

18. 9 12 17 21 24 →

A. 25 B. 27 C. 29 D. 31 E. 33

Answer: __________

STOP!

Figure Matrices

Directions

In the Figure Matrices subtest, each question is a matrix or grid divided into sections. Each section contains either a shape, figure, or question mark. Students must determine which of the five available answers would best replace the question mark to complete the matrix. Questions usually come it two types: Figure Analogy or Pattern Completion.

Sample Questions

1. Figure Analogy

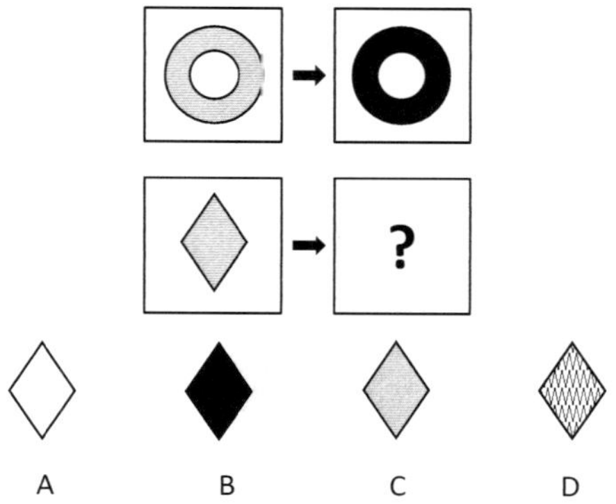

The correct answer is B. B is the answer you would mark on the bubble test form or in the available answer field*.

2. Pattern Completion

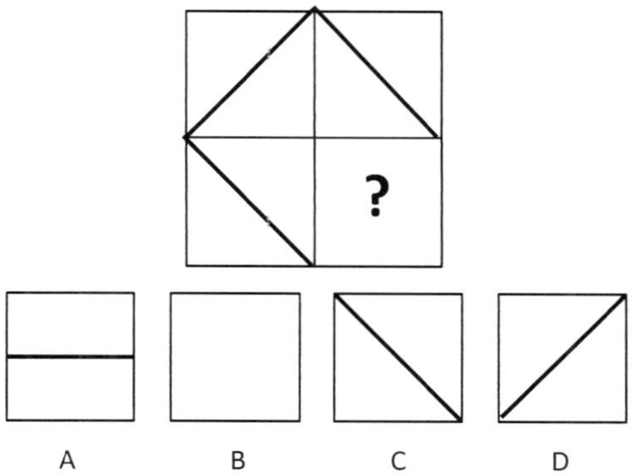

The correct answer is D. D is the answer you would mark on the bubble test form or in the available answer field*.

* Answer fields will not be in your child's exam workbook. Bubble test forms are typically used during the exam and marking your answers on a bubble test form as they do the practice test is recommended.

1.

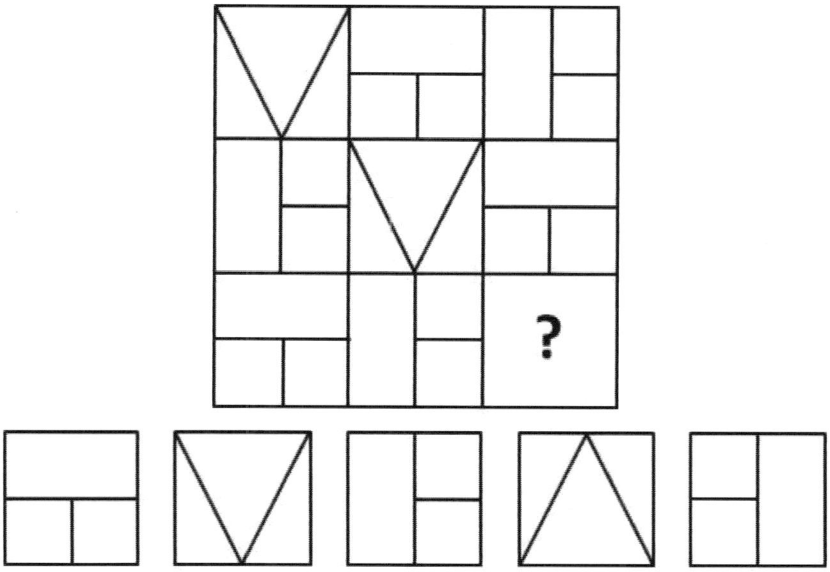

A B C D E

Answer: __________

2.

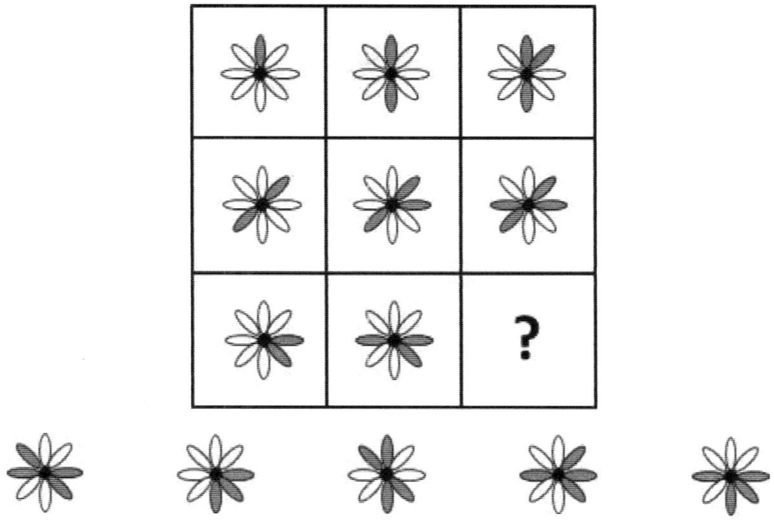

A B C D E

Answer: __________

Continue

3.

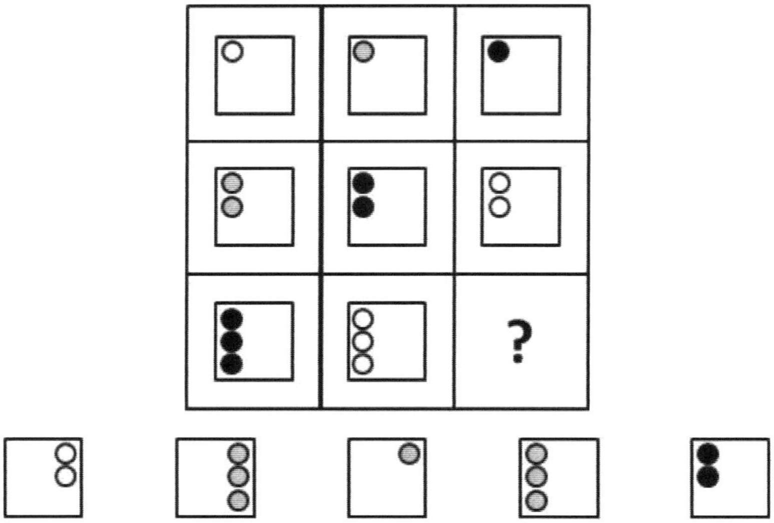

A B C D E

Answer: __________

4.

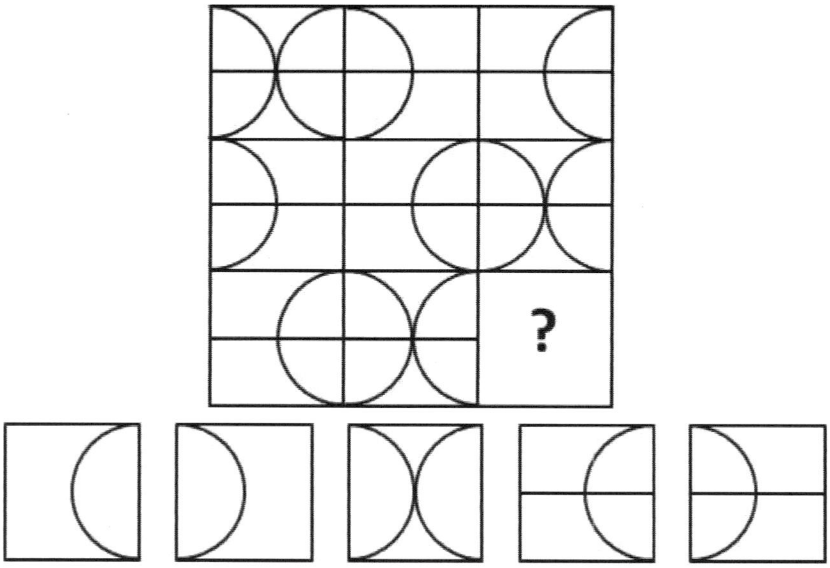

A B C D E

Answer: __________

Continue

5.

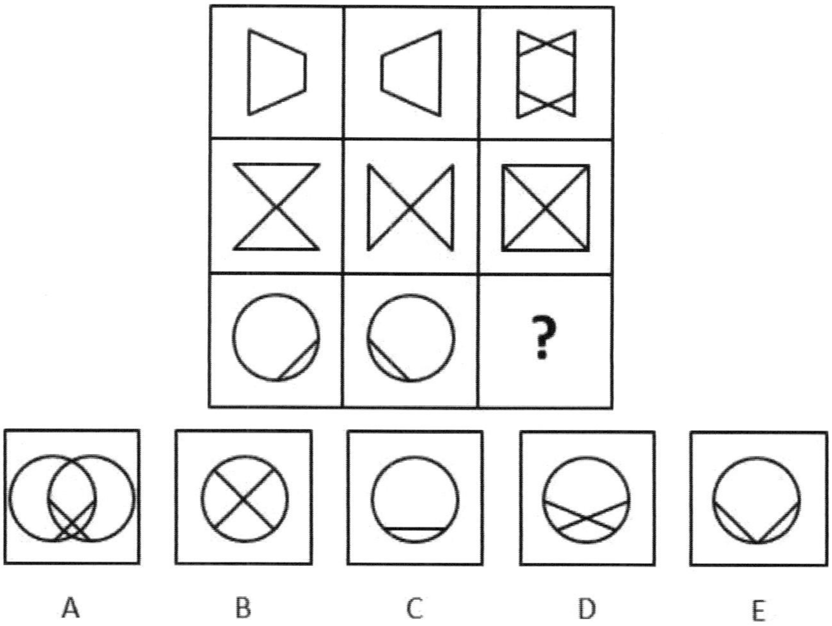

Answer: __________

6.

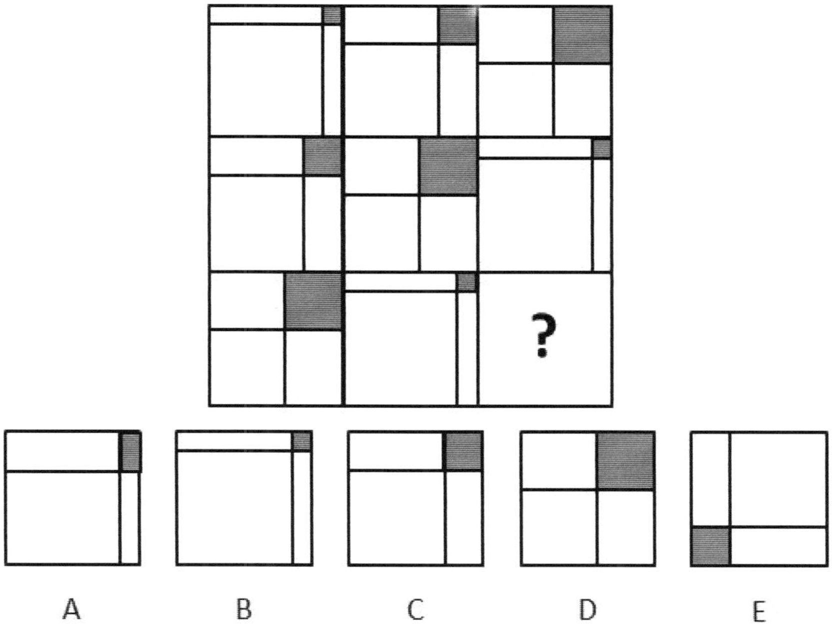

Answer: __________

Continue

7.

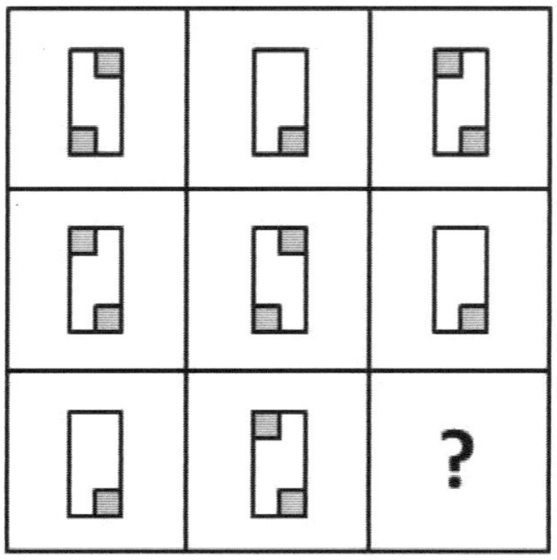

A B C D E

Answer: __________

8.

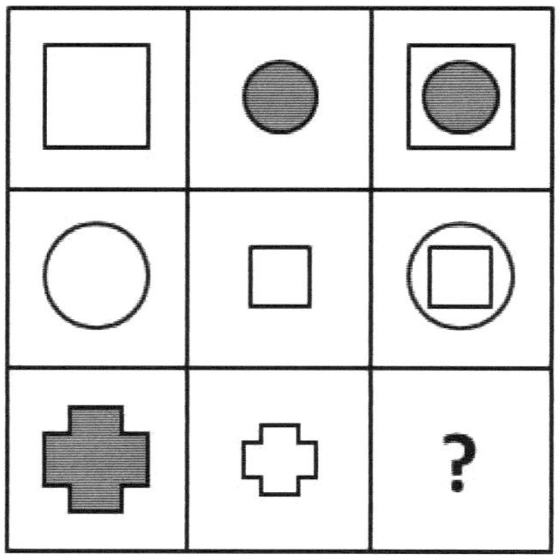

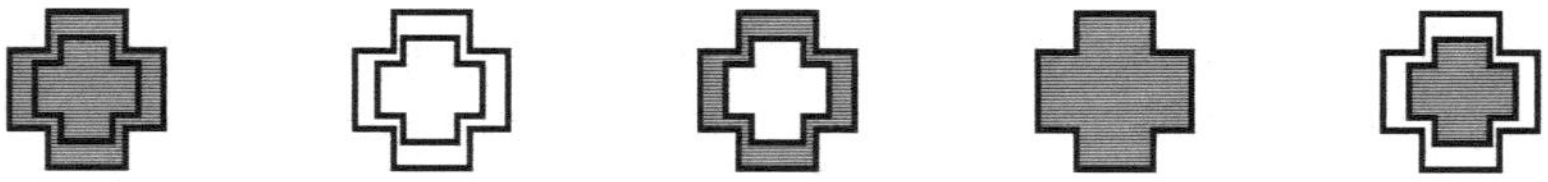

A B C D E

Answer: __________

Continue

9.

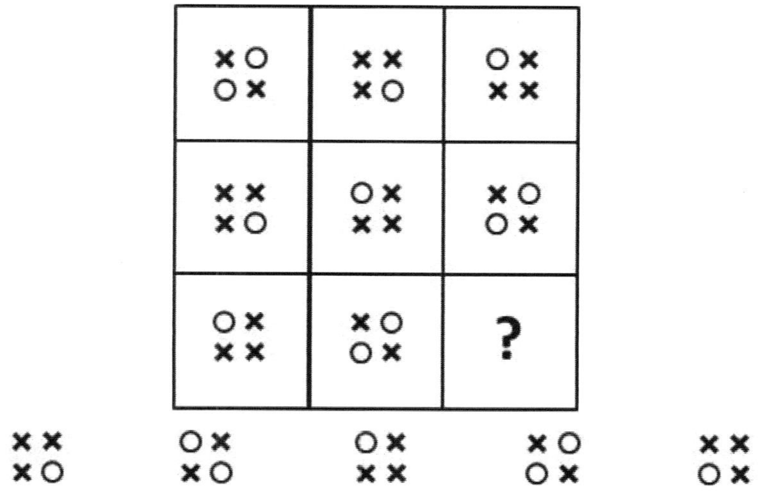

A B C D E

Answer: __________

10.

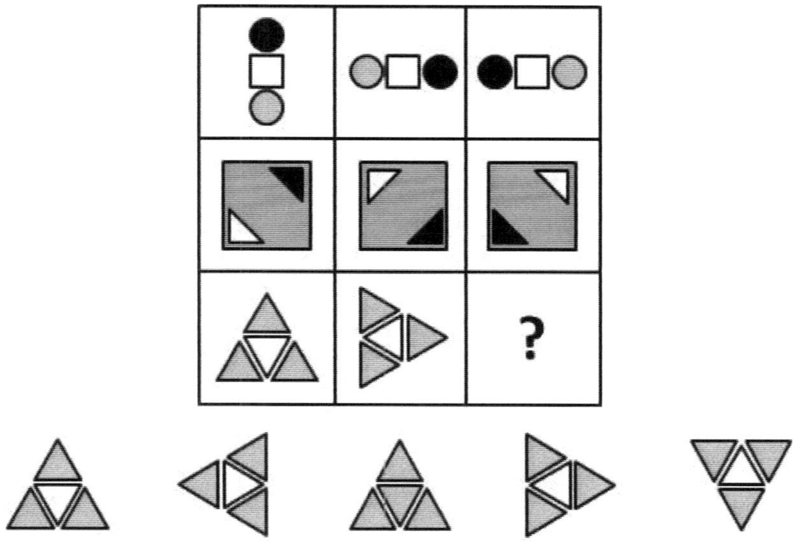

A B C D E

Answer: __________

Continue

11.

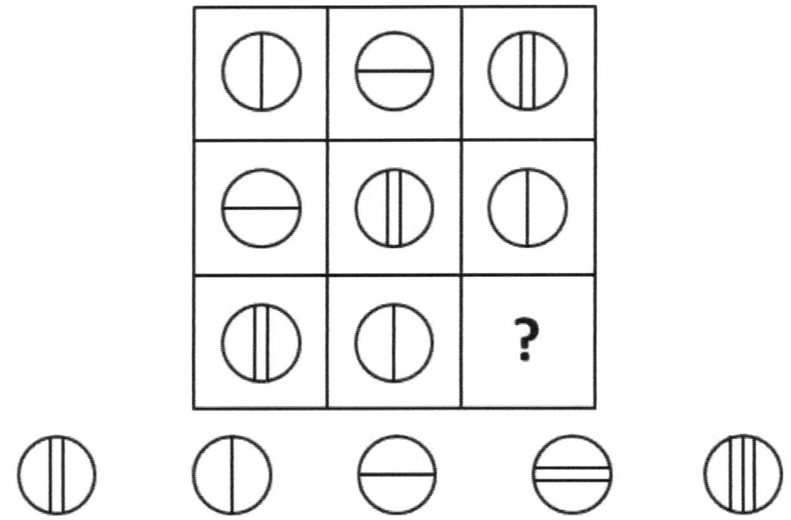

A B C D E

Answer: __________

12.

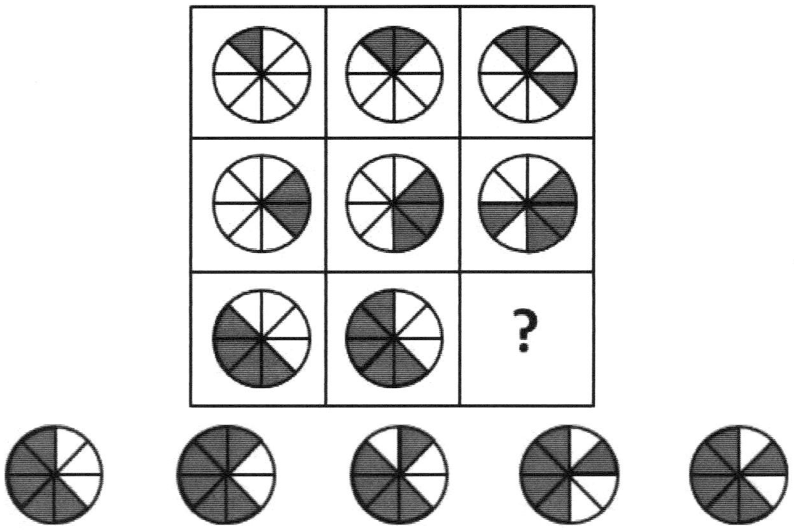

A B C D E

Answer: __________

Continue

13.

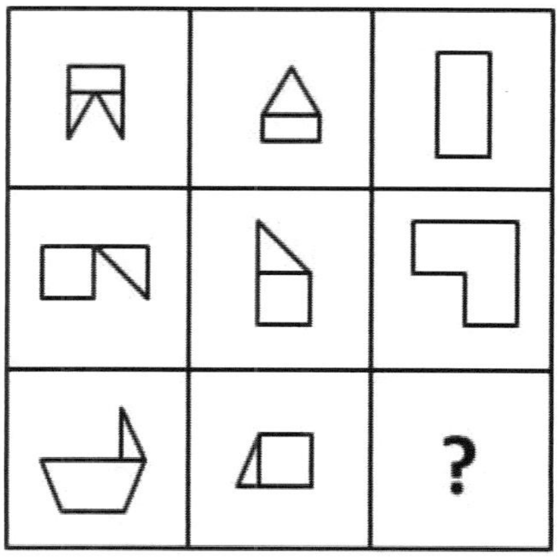

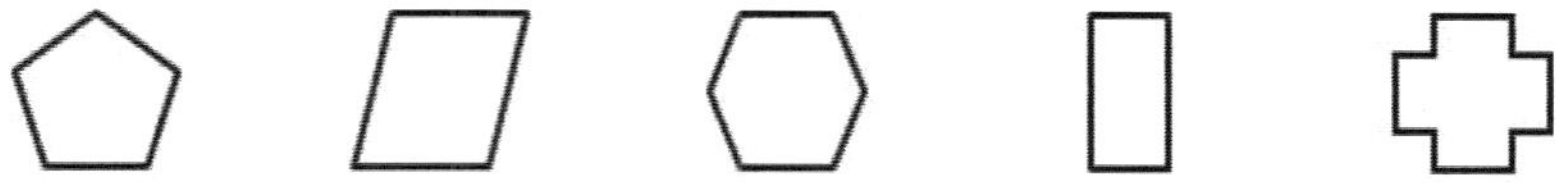

A B C D E

Answer: __________

14.

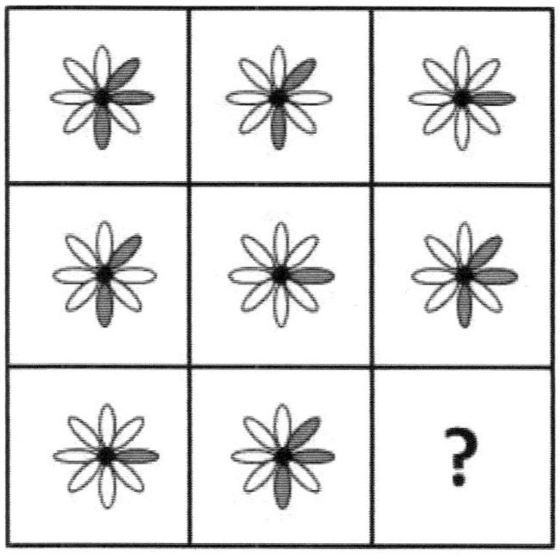

A B C D E

Answer: __________

Continue

15.

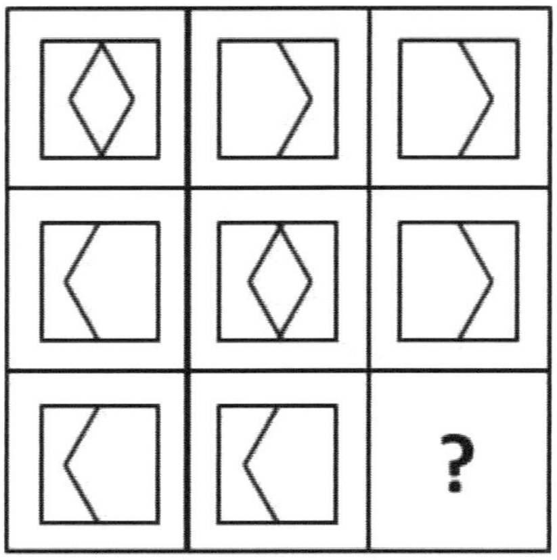

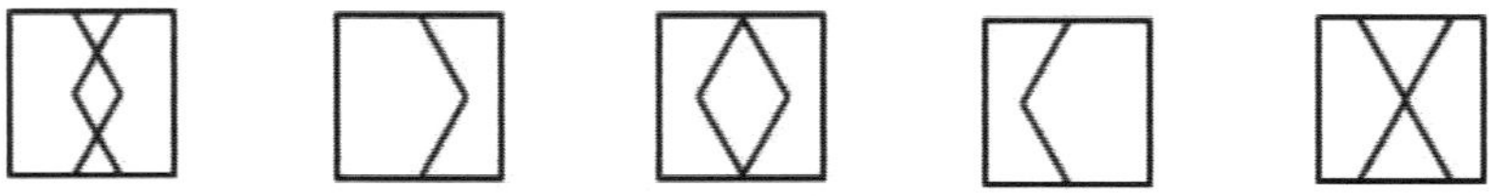

A B C D E

Answer: _________

16.

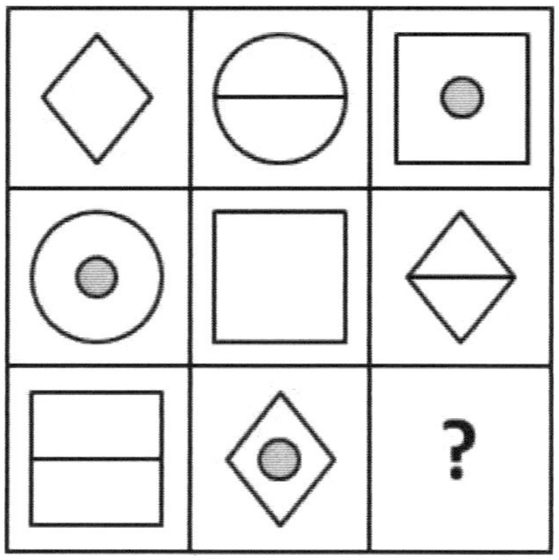

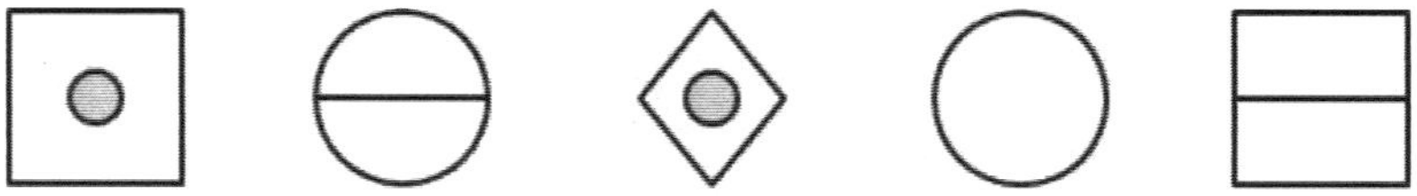

A B C D E

Answer: _________

Continue

17.

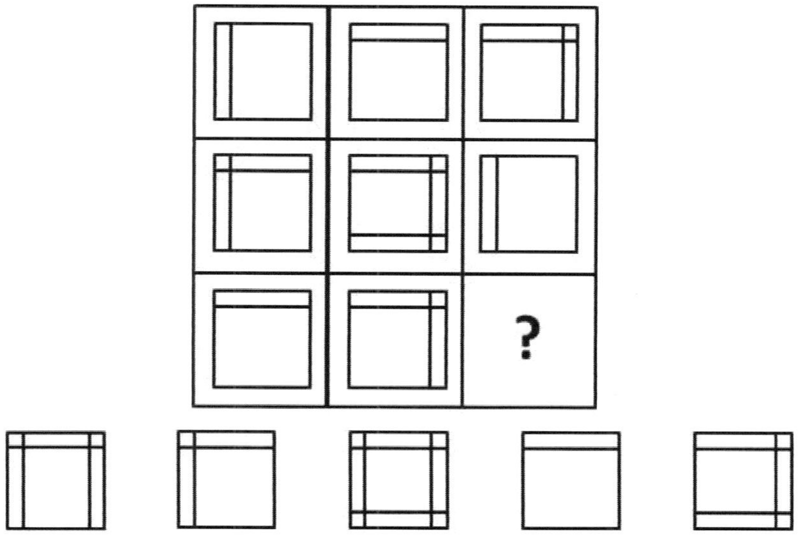

A B C D E

Answer: _________

18.

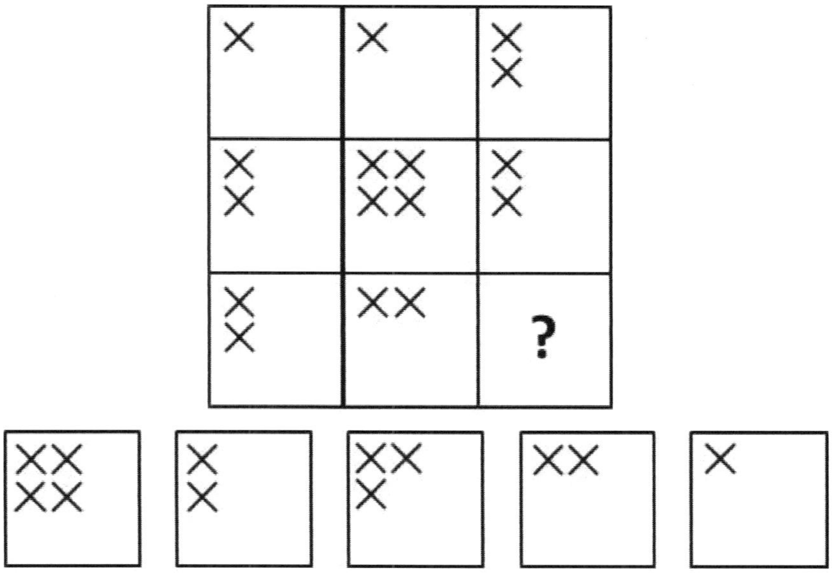

A B C D E

Answer: _________

Continue

19.

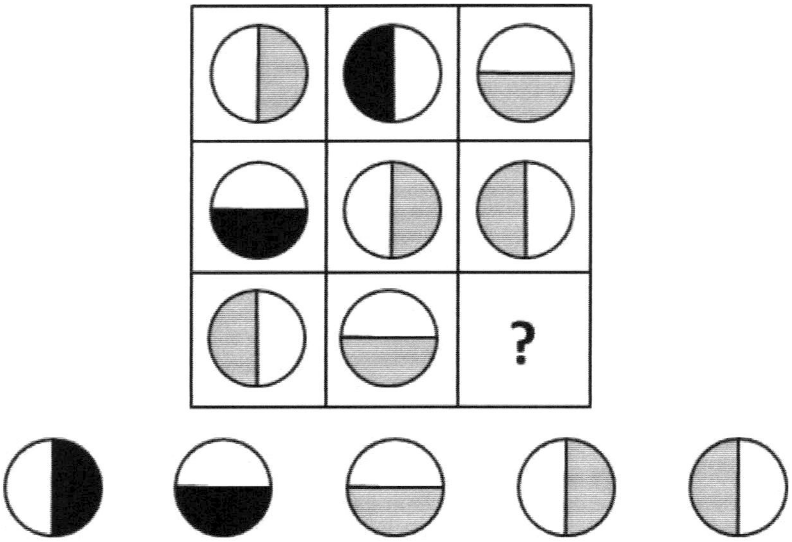

A B C D E

Answer: __________

20.

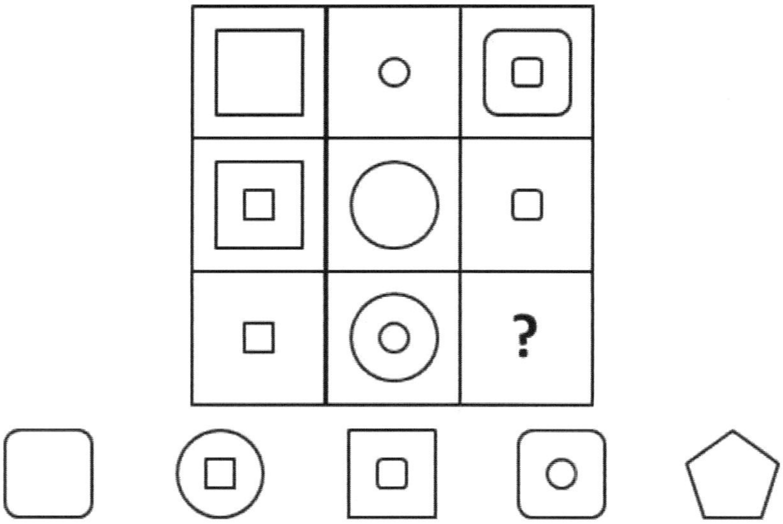

A B C D E

Answer: __________

Continue

21.

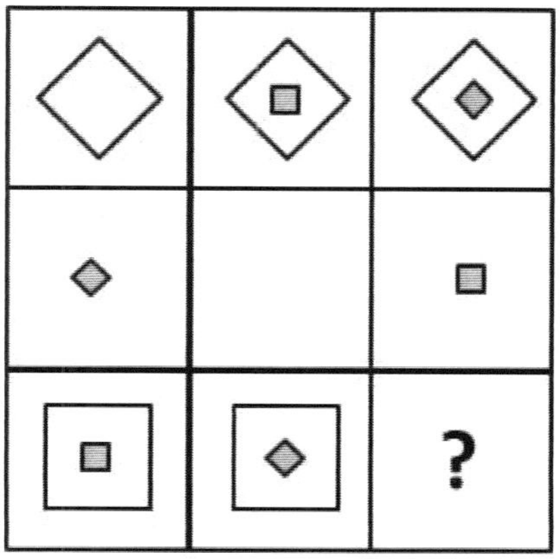

A B C D E

Answer: __________

22.

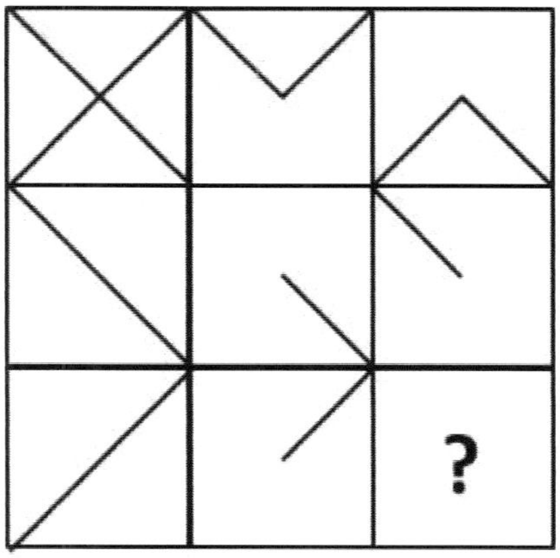

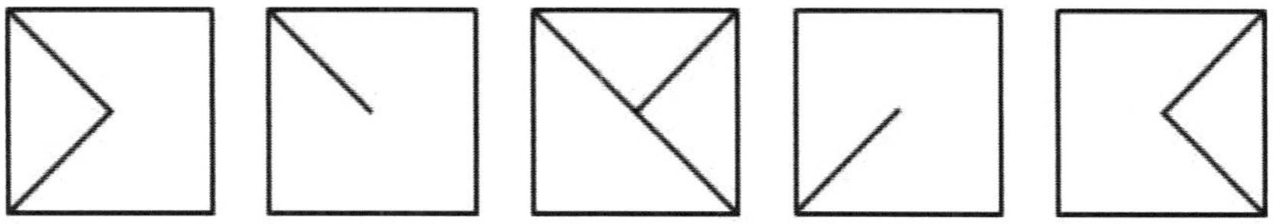

A B C D E

Answer: __________

STOP!

Paper Folding

Directions

In the Paper Folding subtest, each question shows a square piece of paper being folded and then the folded paper is hole-punched. Select the answer from the bottom row that shows how the folded paper with holes will look when it is unfolded.

Sample Question

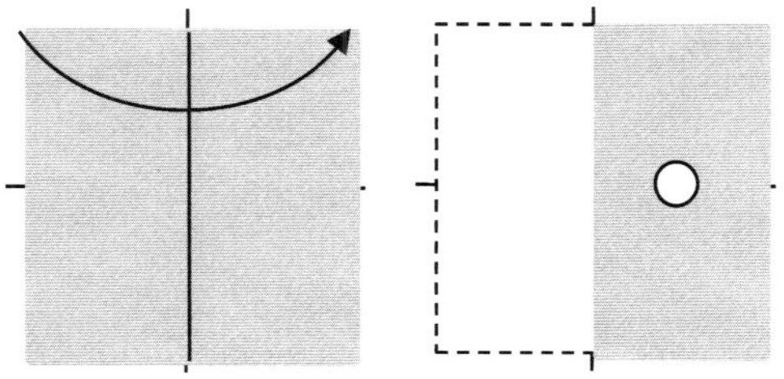

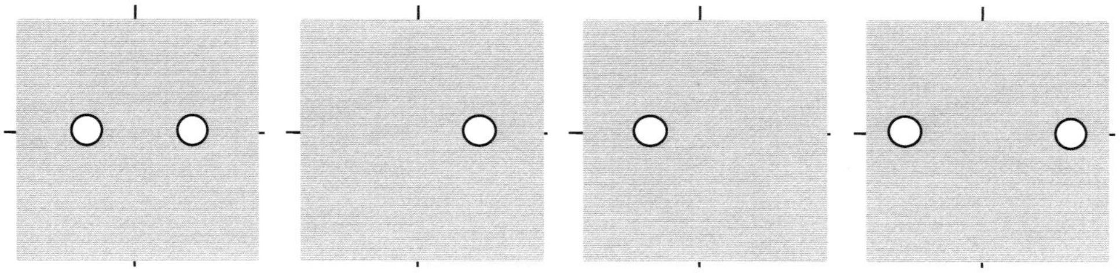

A B C D

The correct answer is A. A is the answer you would mark on the bubble test form or in the available answer field*.

* Answer fields will not be in your child's exam workbook. Bubble test forms are typically used during the exam and marking your answers on a bubble test form as they do the practice test is recommended.

Begin

1.

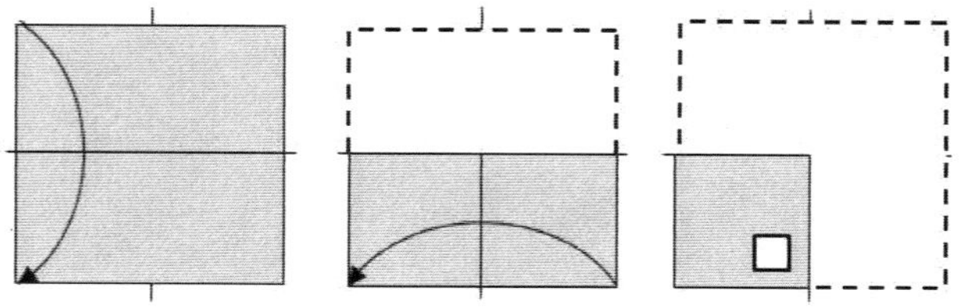

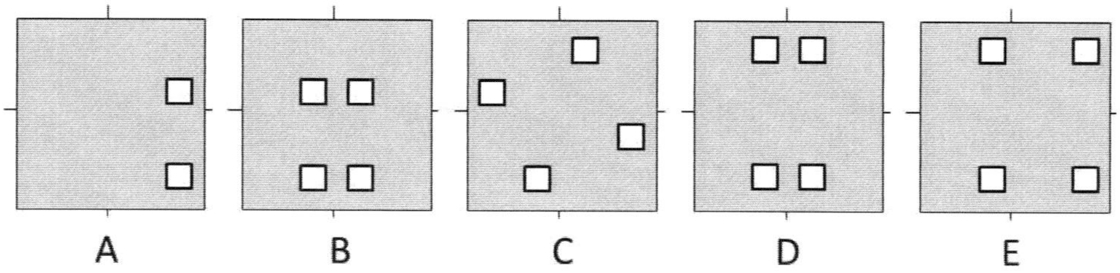

Answer: _________

2.

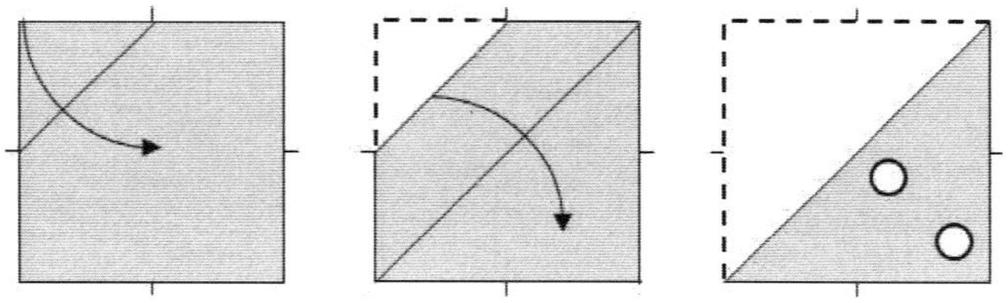

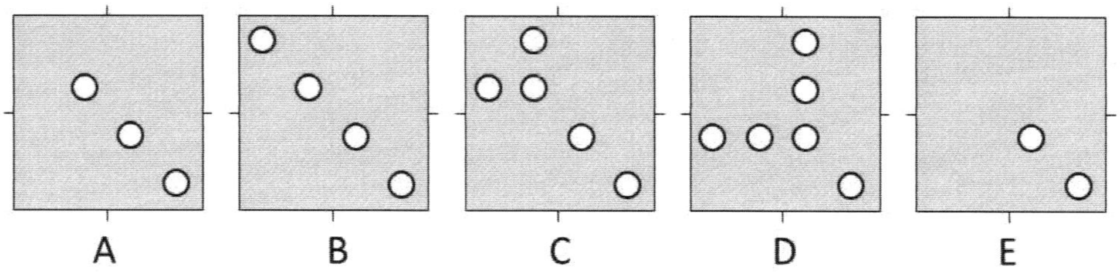

Answer: _________

Continue

3.

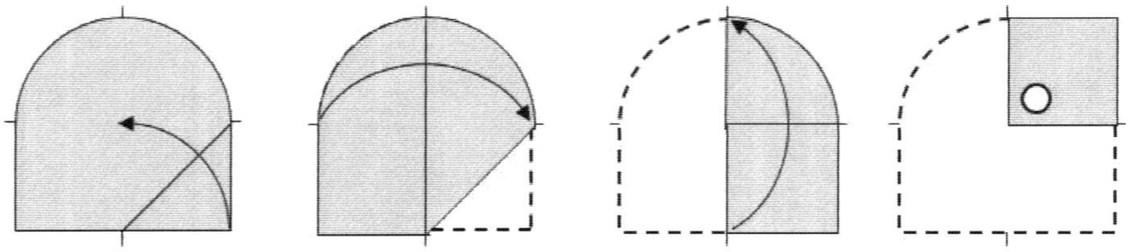

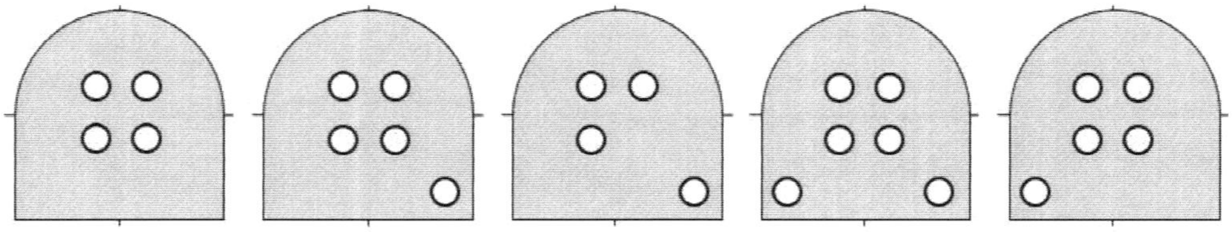

A B C D E

Answer: _________

4.

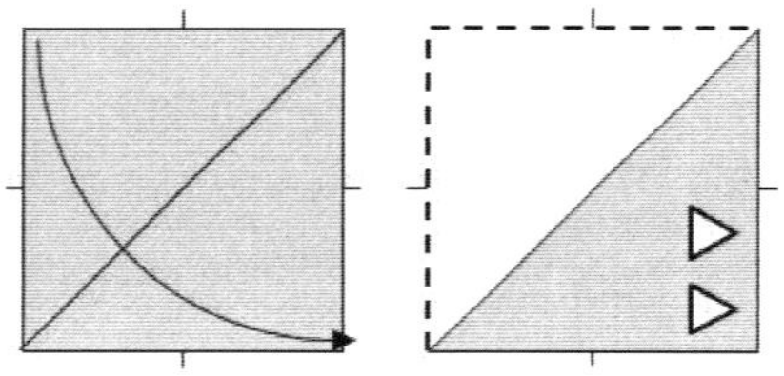

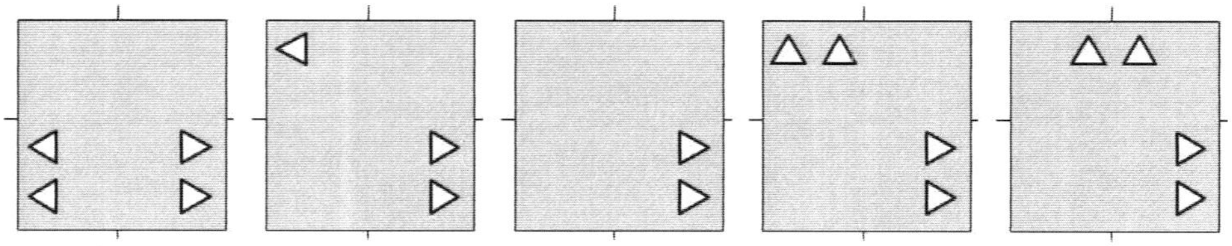

A B C D E

Answer: _________

Continue

5.

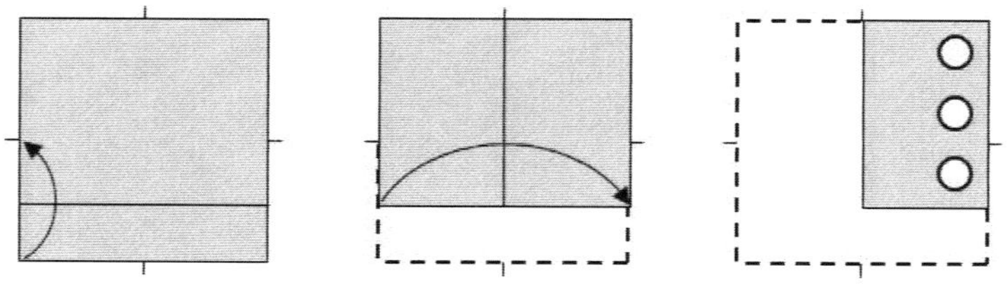

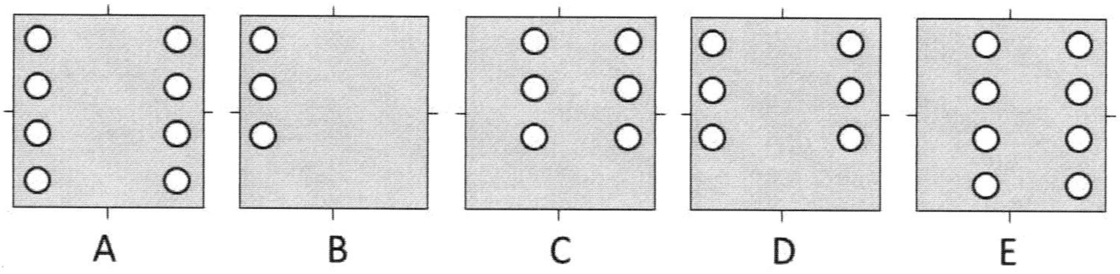

Answer: _________

6.

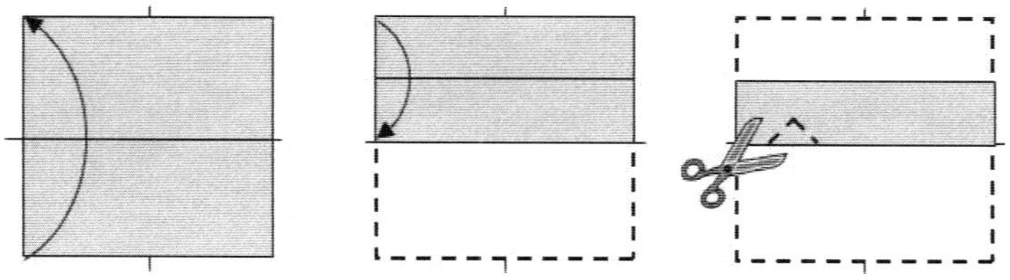

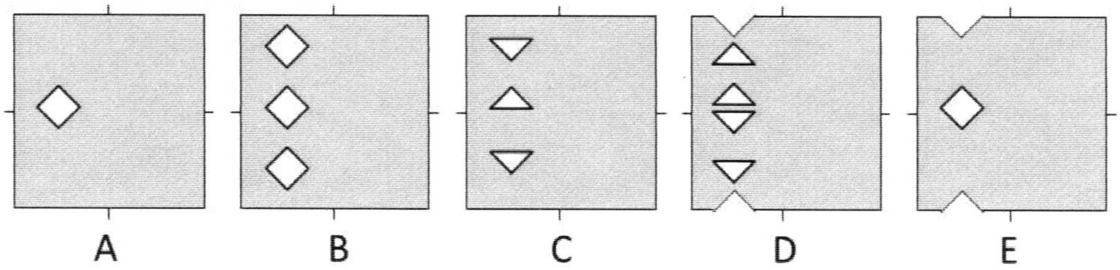

Answer: _________

Continue

7.

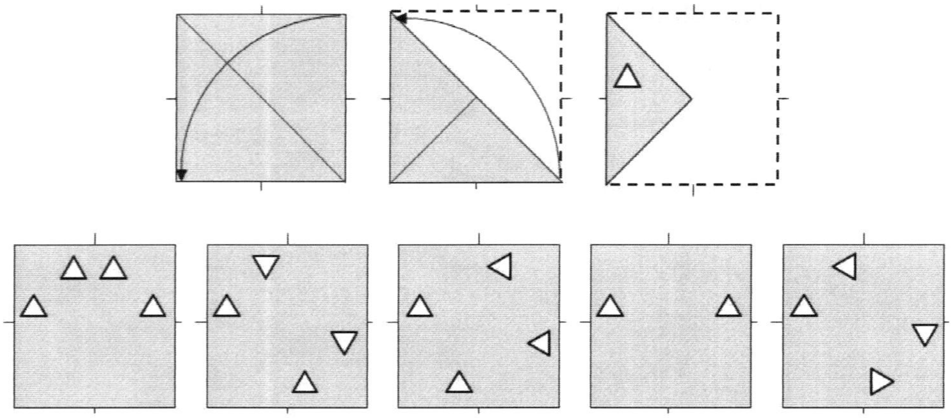

A B C D E

Answer: _________

8.

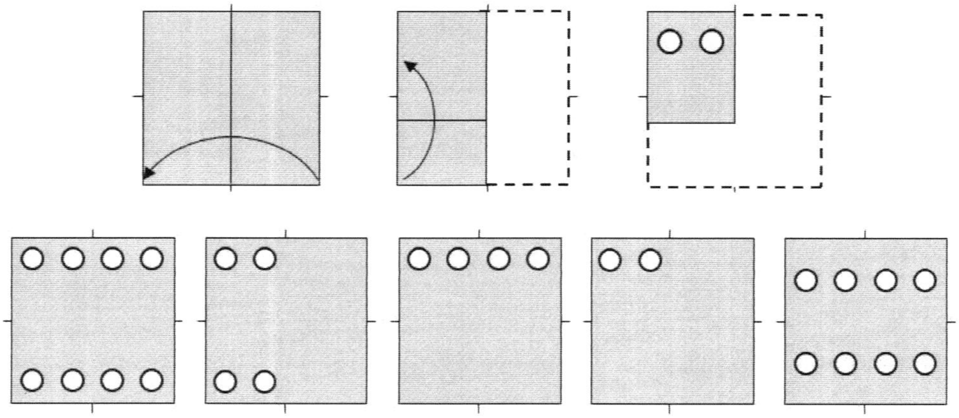

A B C D E

Answer: _________

Continue

9.

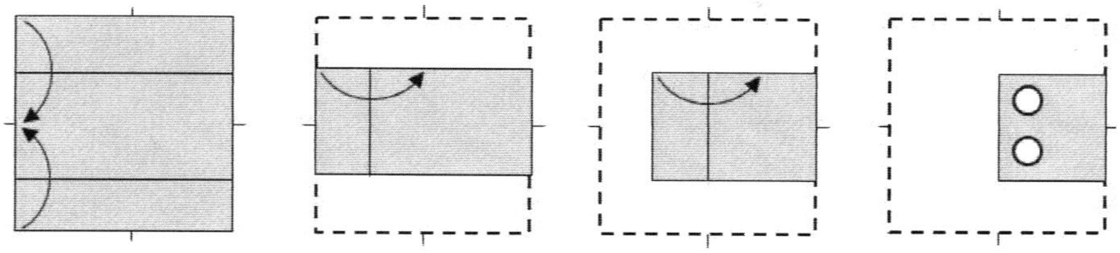

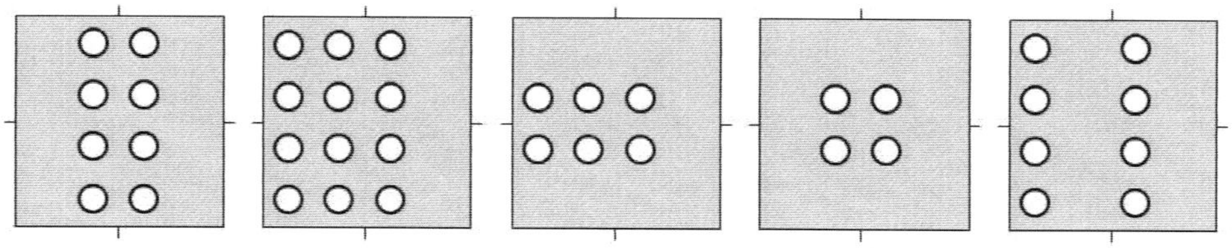

A B C D E

Answer: __________

10.

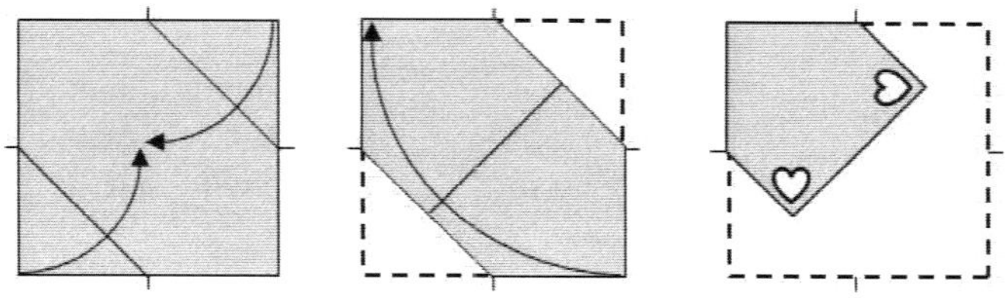

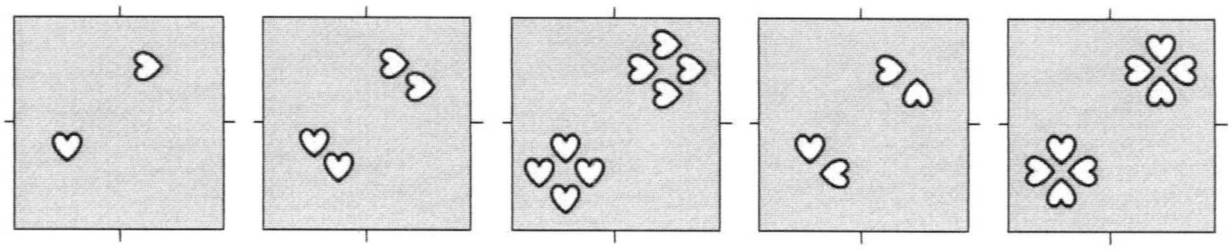

A B C D E

Answer: __________

Continue

11.

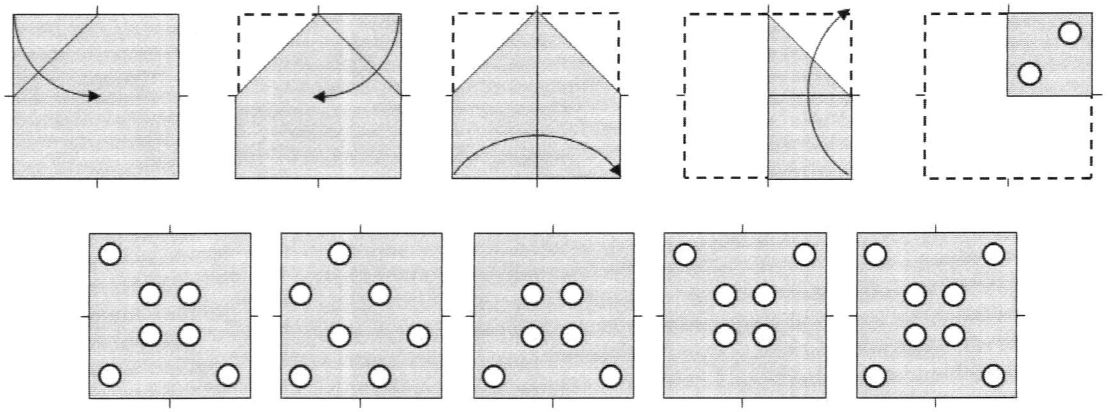

A B C D E

Answer: _________

12.

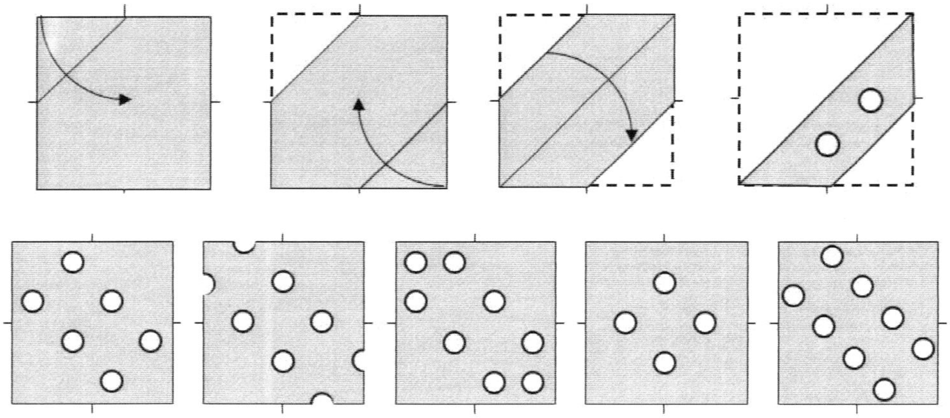

A B C D E

Answer: _________

Continue

13.

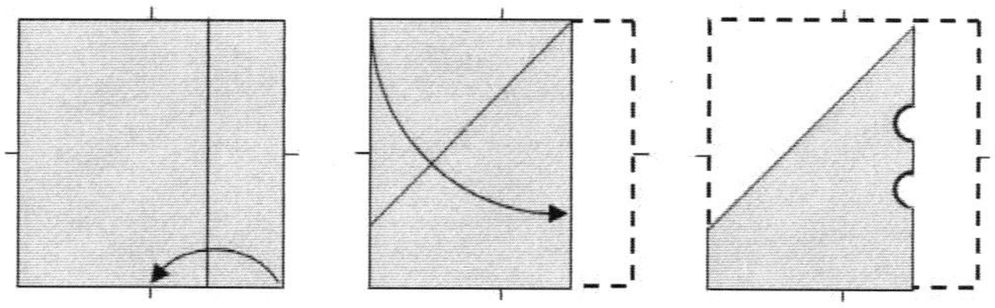

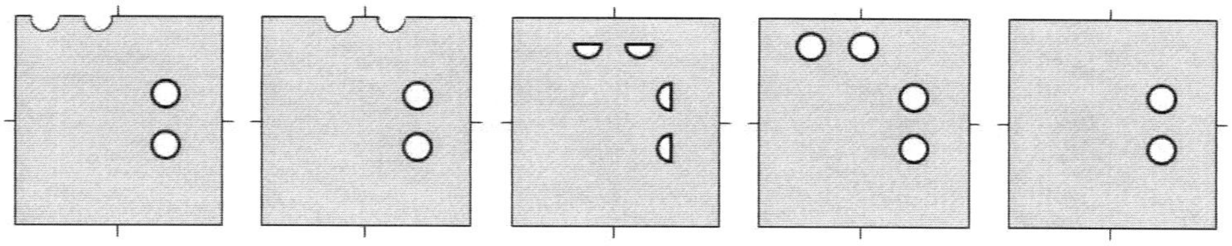

A B C D E

Answer: __________

14.

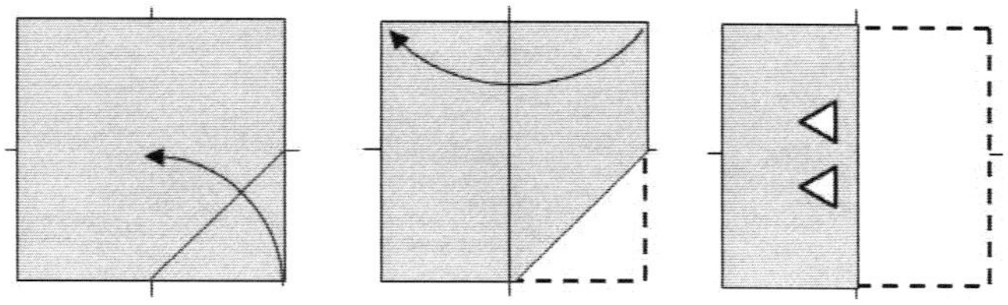

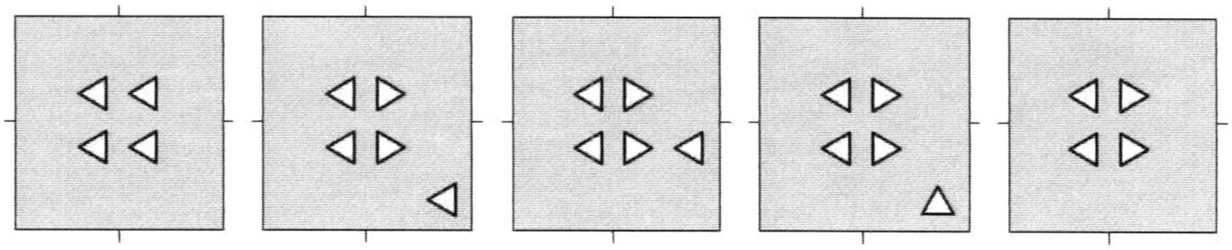

A B C D E

Answer: __________

Continue

15.

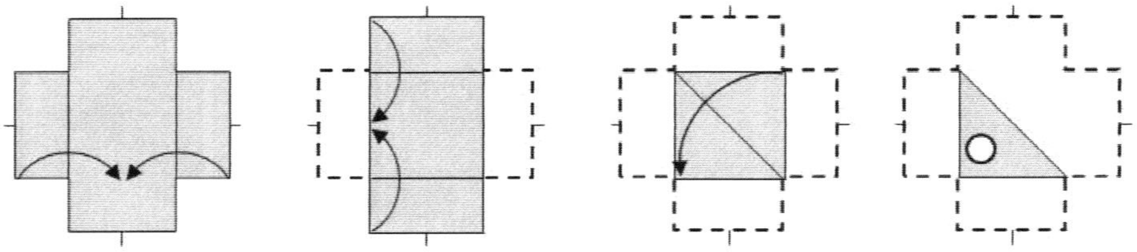

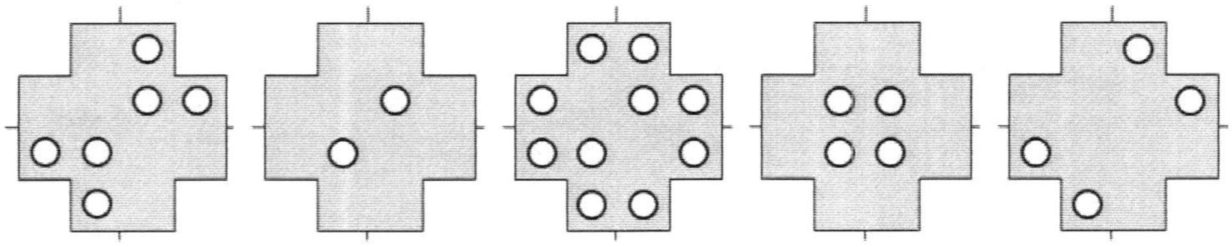

A B C D E

Answer: _________

16.

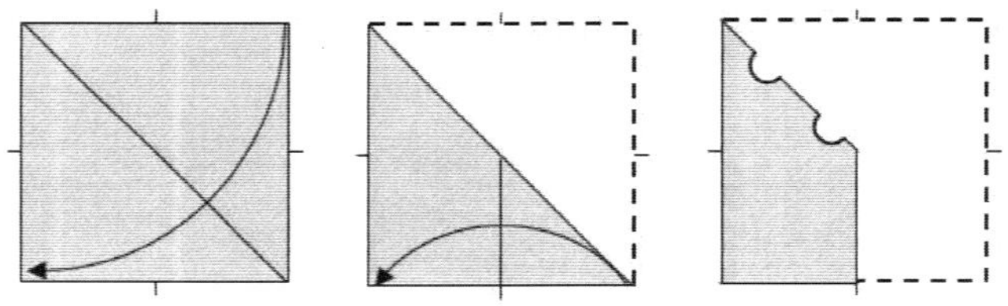

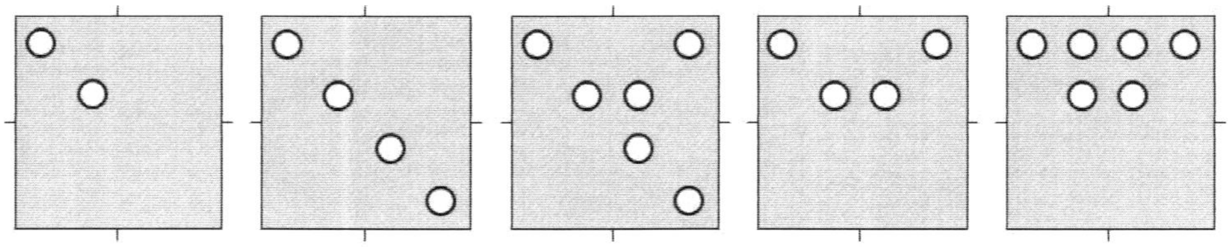

A B C D E

Answer: _________

Figure Classification

Directions

In the Figure Classification subtest, each question has two rows of figures. In the top row, the student is given a set of three figures that are similar in some way. Students must determine how they are similar and then select the figure from the five available answers that is most similar to the pictures on the top row.

Sample Question

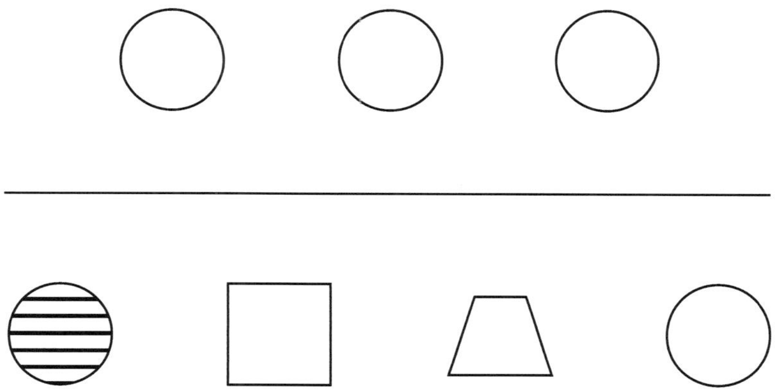

A B C D

The correct answer is D, the white circle. D is the answer you would mark on the bubble test form or in the available answer field*.

* Answer fields will not be in your child's exam workbook. Bubble test forms are typically used during the exam and marking your answers on a bubble test form as they do the practice test is recommended.

Begin

1.

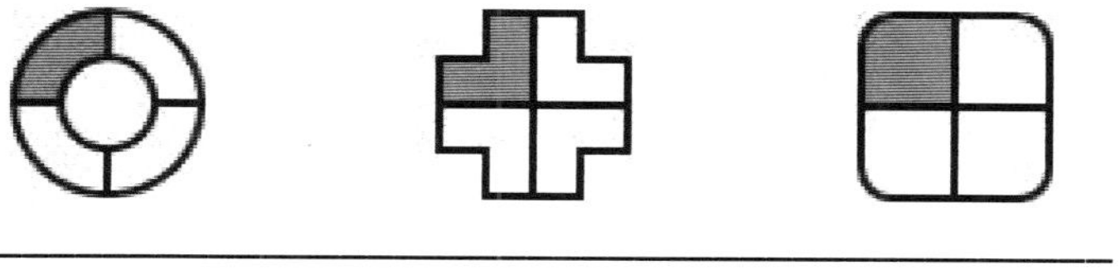

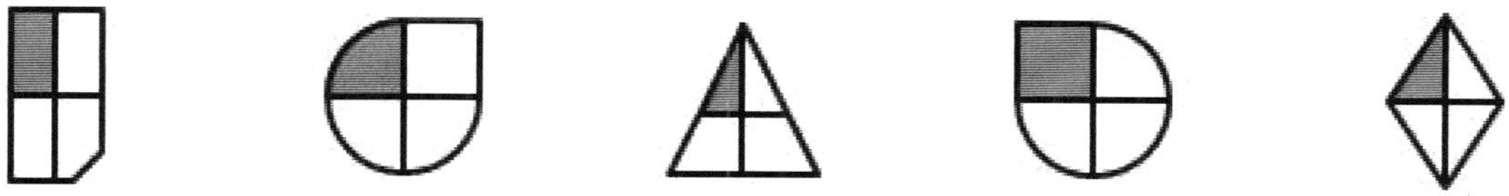

A B C D E

Answer: __________

2.

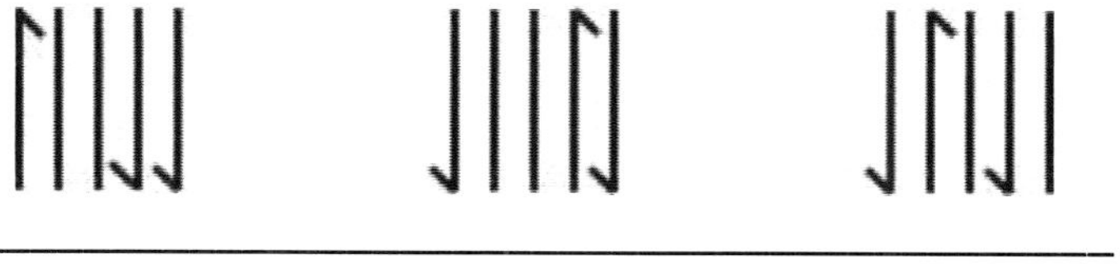

A B C D E

Answer: __________

Continue

3.

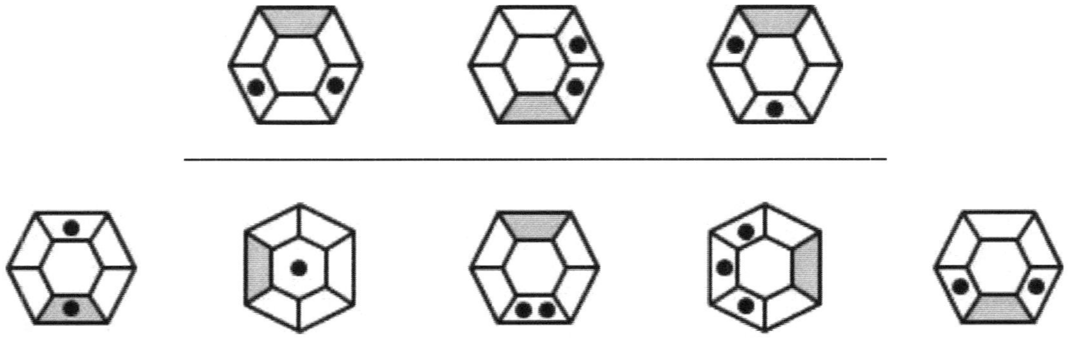

A B C D E

Answer: ________

4.

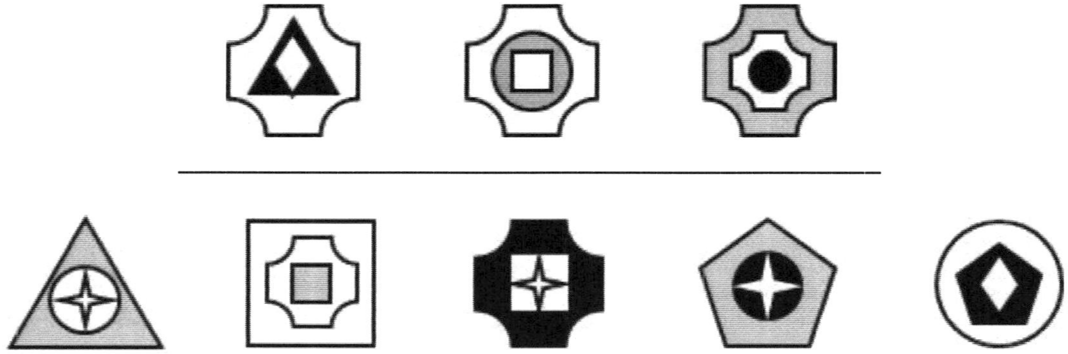

A B C D E

Answer: ________

Continue

5.

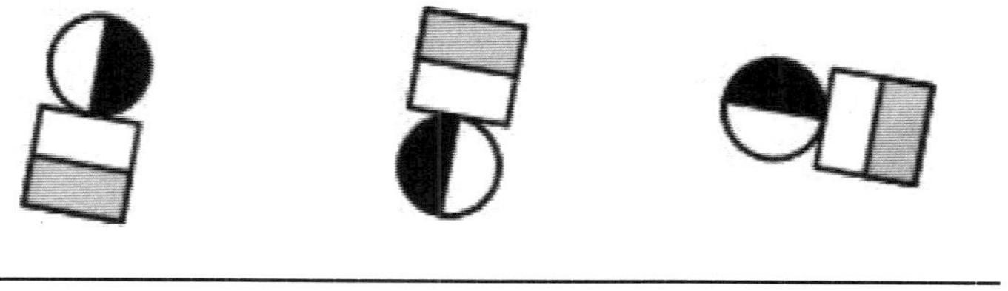

A B C D E

Answer: ________

6.

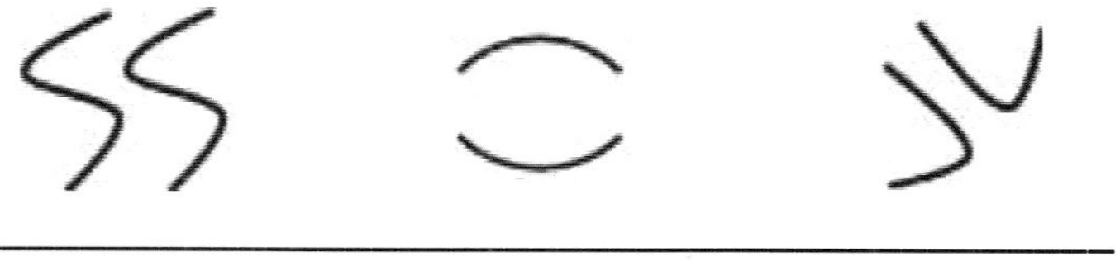

A B C D E

Answer: ________

Continue

7.

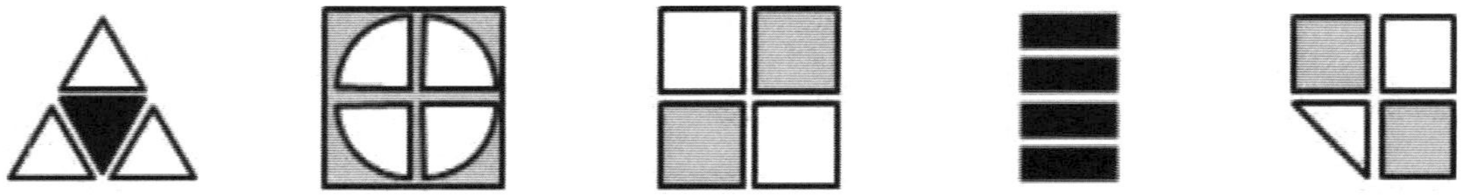

A B C D E

Answer: ________

8.

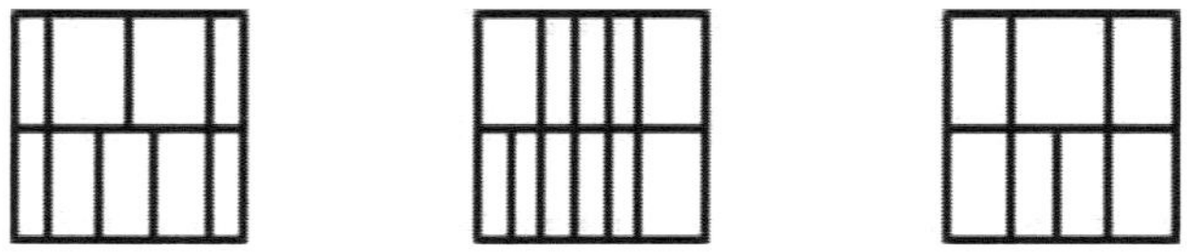

A B C D E

Answer: ________

Continue

9.

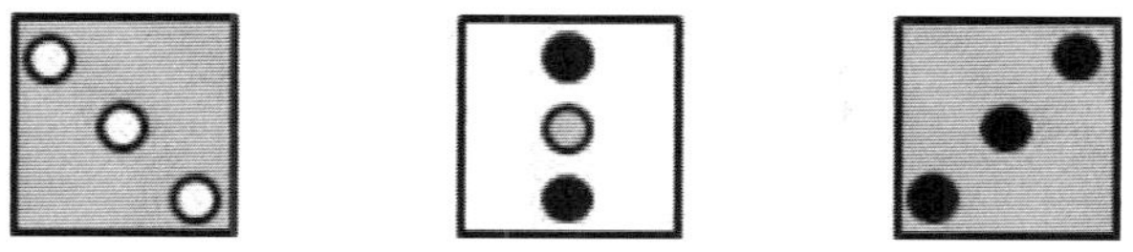

A B C D E

Answer: __________

10.

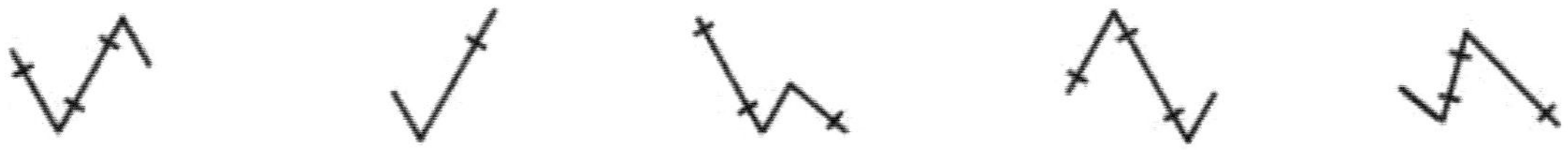

A B C D E

Answer: __________

Continue

11.

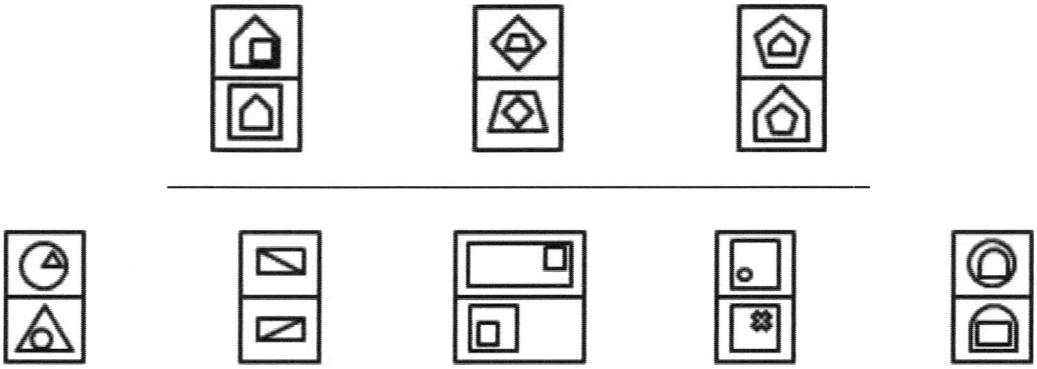

A B C D E

Answer: __________

12.

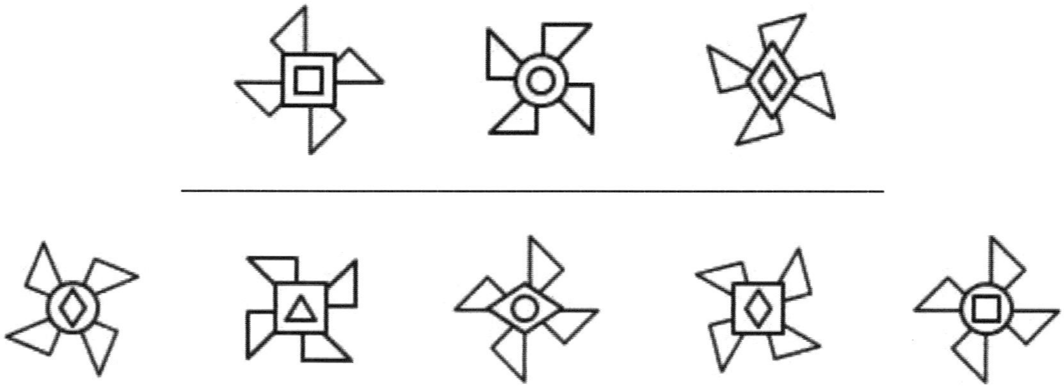

A B C D E

Answer: __________

Continue

13.

A B C D E

Answer: __________

14.

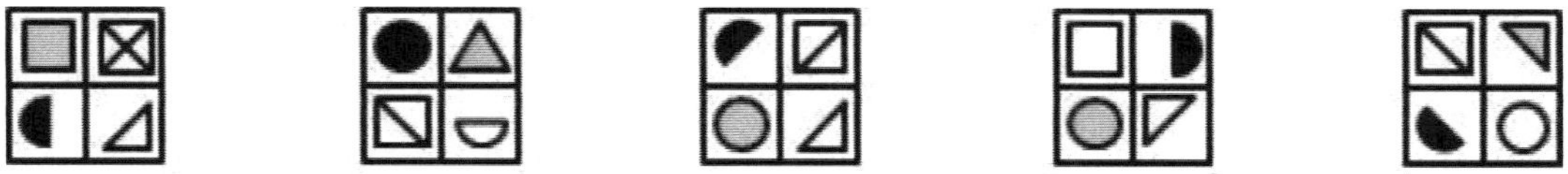

A B C D E

Answer: __________

Continue

15.

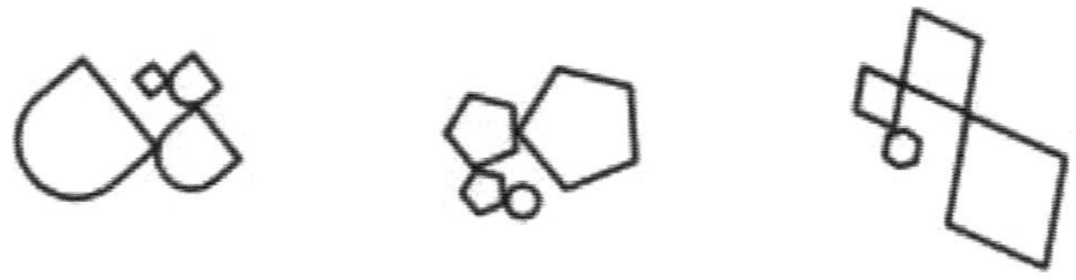

A B C D E

Answer: ________

16.

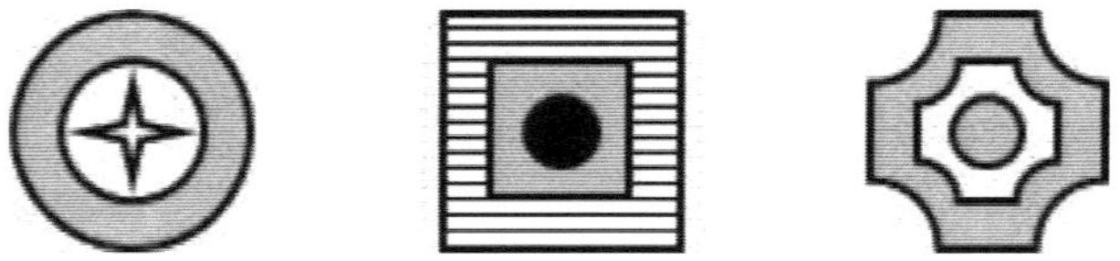

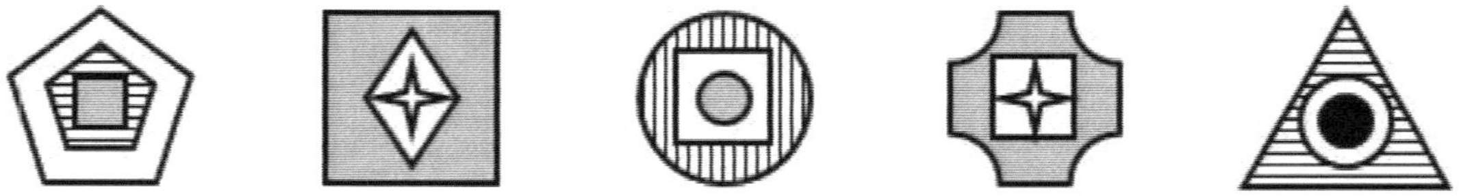

A B C D E

Answer: ________

Continue

17.

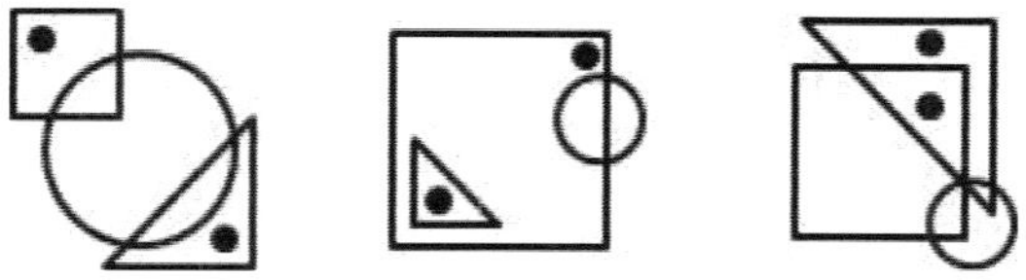

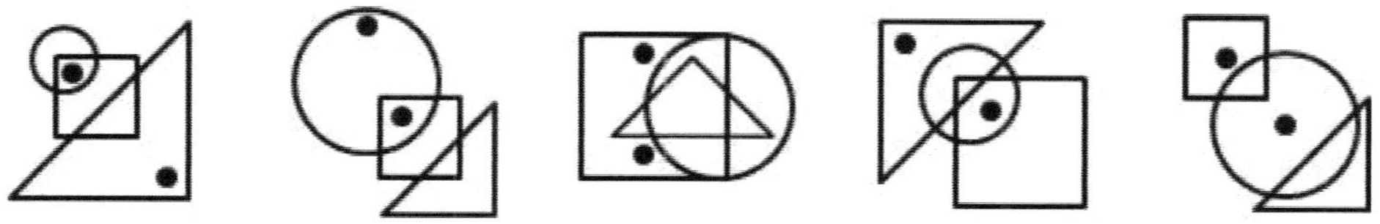

A B C D E

Answer: __________

18.

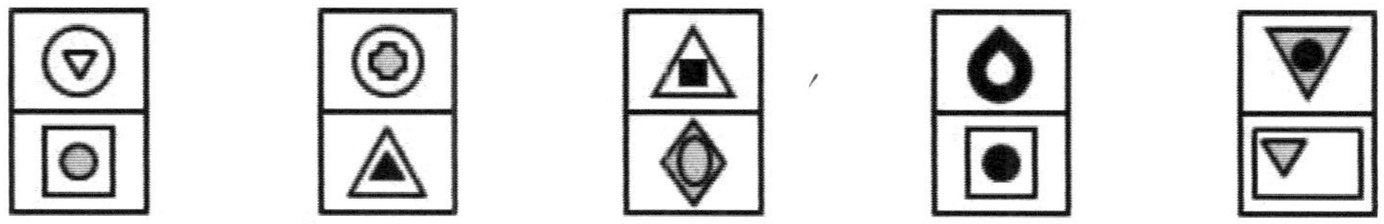

A B C D E

Answer: __________

Continue

19.

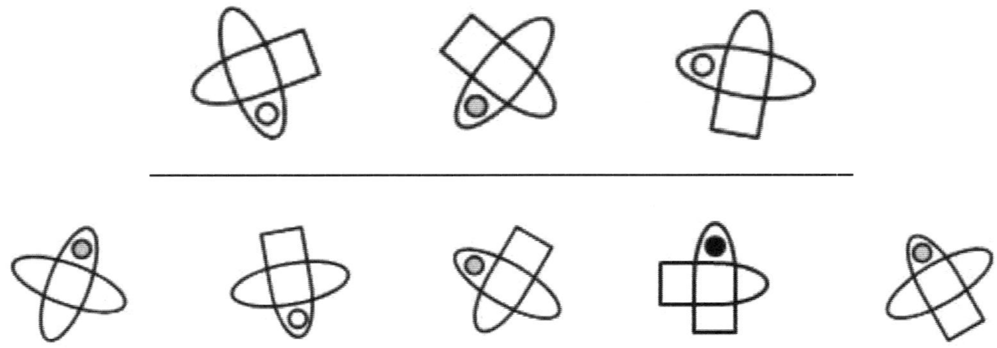

A B C D E

Answer: _________

20.

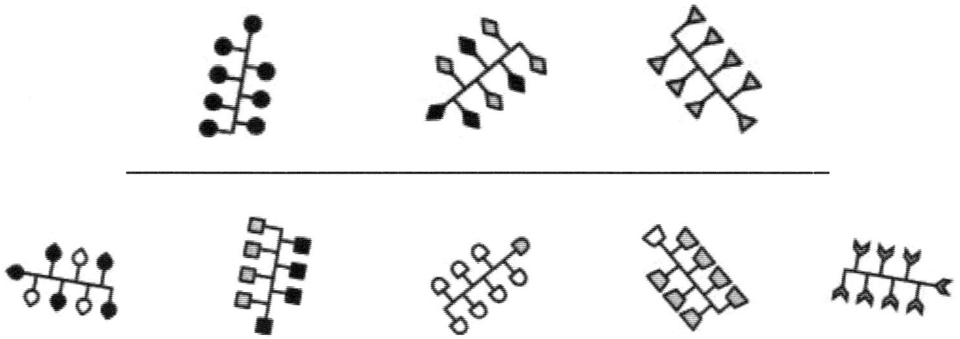

A B C D E

Answer: _________

Continue

21.

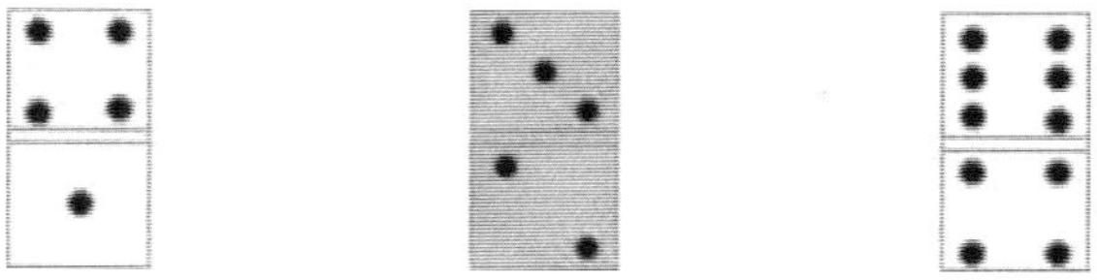

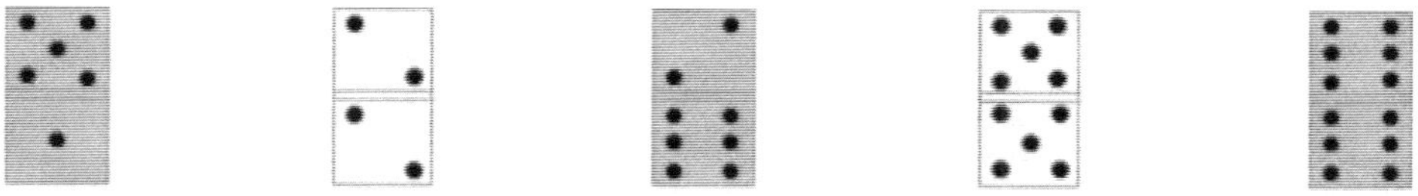

A B C D E

Answer: __________

22.

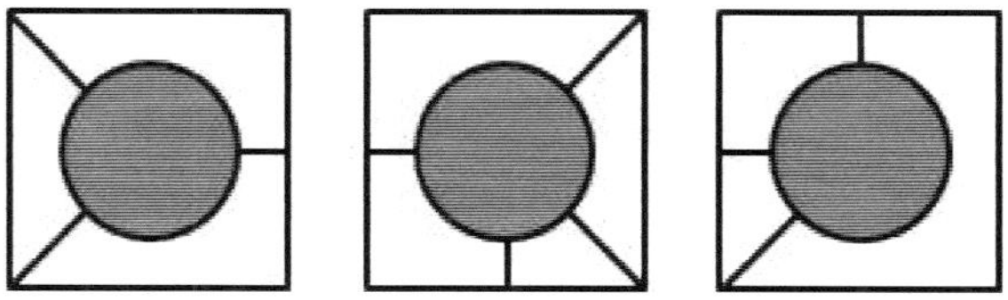

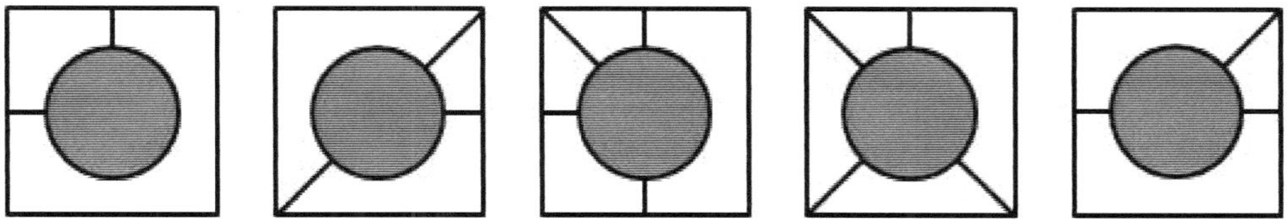

A B C D E

Answer: __________

STOP!

Practice Test 2
Answers

Verbal Analogies

1.	D	tree	A rose is a type of flower and an oak is a type of tree.
2.	B	water	A brush is used to apply paint and a hose is used to apply water.
3.	D	airplane	Fins help a fish swim and wings help an airplane fly; both relationships are about objects and the part that helps them move.
4.	E	cave	Bees live in a hive and bats [typically] live in a cave.
5.	B	shelf	A dish is stored in a cabinet and a book is stored on a [book]shelf.
6.	B	pitcher	A nostril is found on a nose and a spout is found on a pitcher.
7.	D	dollar	Dude is a slang word for a boy and buck is a slang word for a dollar.
8.	E	internet	A page is found within a book and a website is found within the internet.
9.	C	meat	An almond is a type of nut and pork is a type of meat.
10.	A	robbers	Hide is the opposite of seek and cops is the opposite of robbers.
11.	B	pizza	A jewel is found on a crown and pepperoni is found on a pizza. Although refrigerator could also be correct, it is not the "best" answer as pepperoni is "stored in" not "found on" a refrigerator.
12.	C	bone	A card is a single component of a deck and a bone is a single component of a skeleton.
13.	B	food	When a person is greedy, they want money, and when a person is hungry, they want food.
14.	E	child	Sibling is a gender neutral term for sister and child is the gender neutral daughter.
15.	B	Monday	Tuesday is the day before Wednesday and Monday is the day before Tuesday.
16.	C	ink	A carton is a container for milk and a pen is a container for ink.

17.	D	flood	An insignificant amount of water would be a trickle and a major amount of water would be a flood.
18.	B	radio	A limb is part of a tree and a speaker is part of a radio.
19.	D	cardboard	A tire is made of rubber and a box is usually made from cardboard.
20.	C	book	Sour is a type of taste and novel is a type of book.
21.	E	knob	A pull is the handle on a drawer and a knob is the handle on a door.
22.	C	many	Solitary refers to one or a single item and multitudes refers to a large number or many items.
23.	B	ring	Massages take place in a spa and boxing takes place in a ring.
24.	D	poems	An author writes books and a poet writes poems.

Sentence Completion

1.	C	hurt
2.	A	understand
3.	E	negotiate
4.	B	predicament
5.	B	adjusted
6.	D	surprised
7.	D	illegal
8.	C	stole
9.	E	elevator
10.	B	intelligent
11.	E	thought
12.	C	unacceptable
13.	D	knowledge
14.	B	parallel
15.	B	tomato
16.	D	tablecloth
17.	C	sense
18.	E	come
19.	D	worthless
20.	E	approximate

Verbal Classification

1.	A	pitch	Classification:	Baseball terms.
2.	E	rake	Classification:	Gardening terms.
3.	E	Earth	Classification:	Planets.
4.	C	red velvet	Classification:	Types of cakes.
5.	C	hickory	Classification:	Types of trees.
6.	E	skateboard	Classification:	Things that can be used to get someplace quickly.
7.	E	Spanish	Classification:	Languages.
8.	D	volley	Classification:	Words that can be followed by "ball" to form a team sport.
9.	D	panda	Classification:	Animals that are black and white.
10.	B	ounce	Classification:	Measurements.
11.	E	whistle	Classification:	Instruments/Things that are blown into.
12.	A	variety	Classification:	Synonyms.
13.	A	moon	Classification:	Astronomy terms/Objects formed in space.
14.	B	kidney	Classification:	Organs.
15.	C	carpenter	Classification:	Jobs/Professions associated with building a house.
16.	B	flee	Classification:	Words that mean to move away from.
17.	E	bathroom	Classification:	Rooms in a house.
18.	C	bike	Classification:	Things often found in a garage.
19.	A	mist	Classification:	Precipitation in liquid form not frozen.
20.	C	distress	Classification:	Synonyms.

Number Analogies

1.	D	21	Multiply the first number by 3 to get the second number.
2.	B	6	Subtract 13 from the first number to get the second number.
3.	C	16	Multiply the first number by 3 and add 1 to get the second number.
4.	E	14	Divide the first number by 2 to get the second number.
5.	E	22	Divide the first number by 5 to get the second number.
6.	C	5	Divide the first number by 3 to get the second number.
7.	D	21	Multiply the first number by 3 to get the second number.
8.	C	12	Add 7 to the first number to get the second number.
9.	A	16	Multiply the first number by 2 and subtract 2 to get the second number.
10.	B	20	Add 13 to the first number to get the second number.
11.	D	5	Divide the first number by 2 and subtract 1 to get the second number.
12.	E	4	Subtract 8 from the first number to get the second number.
13.	C	37	Multiply the first number by 3 and add 4 to get the second number.
14.	B	9	Subtract 12 from the first number to get the second number.
15.	D	11	Multiply the first number by 2 and subtract 5 to get the second number.
16.	C	4	Divide the first number by 3 and add 1 to get the second number.
17.	D	33	Multiply the first number by 4 and add 1 to get the second number.
18.	B	16	Multiply the first number by 3 and subtract 2 to get the second number.

Number Puzzles

1.	E	56
2.	C	3
3.	C	56
4.	A	6
5.	B	9
6.	D	14
7.	C	3
8.	C	3
9.	A	7
10.	B	36
11.	A	4
12.	B	22
13.	C	30
14.	A	0
15.	D	18
16.	B	14

Number Series

1.	C	9	Add 3 to the first number to get the second number, subtract 1 from the second number to get the third. Repeat starting with the third number.
2.	A	23	Subtract 4 from the first number to get the second number, add 2 to the second number to get the third. Repeat starting with the third number.
3.	D	1	Decreasing subtraction - -5 -4 -3 -2. Subtract 5 from the first number to get the second. Subtract 4 from the second number to get the third. Decrease the number to subtract by 1 each time.
4.	D	17	Add 1 to the first number to get the second number, add 2 the second number to get the third. Repeat starting with the third number.
5.	C	20	Increasing addition - 1, 2, 3, 4. Add 1 to the first number to get the second. Add 2 to the second number to get the third. Increase the number to add by one each time.
6.	E	28	Every other number. Each odd number has 3 is added to the previous odd number to get the next. The even numbers use decreasing subtraction - -5 -4 -3 -2. Subtract 5 from the first even number to get the second even number. Subtract 4 from the second even number to get the third. Decrease the number to subtract by 1 each time.
7.	B	11	Subtract 2 from the first number to get the second number, add 3 to the second number to get the third. Repeat starting with the third number.
8.	A	75	Increasing addition - 1 2 3 5 7 11 13 (prime numbers). Add 1 to the first number to get the second. Add 2 to the second number to get the third. Increase the number to the next prime number each time.
9.	E	34	Increasing addition - 4, 5, 6, 7. Add 4 to the first number to get the second. Add 5 to the second number to get the third. Increase the number to add by one each time.
10.	B	14	Pattern of the numbers. – Reverse the order of the first three numbers starting with the fourth number.

11.	D	8	Decreasing subtraction - 24 12 6. Subtract 24 from the first number to get the second number. Subtract 12 from the second number to get the third. Decrease the number to subtract in half each time.
12.	E	4	Divide the first number by 4 to get the second number, divide the second number by 2 to get the third. Repeat starting with the third number.
13.	B	1	Sets of 2 - Square the first number in each set (multiply it by itself) to get the second number of each set. Then subtract 1 from the first number in the set to get the first number of the next set (the third number). Repeat starting with the third number.
14.	A	3	Sets of 3 – Add 2 to the first number to get the second and add 0 to the second number to get the third (completing the first set of 3). Then subtract 4 from the first number in first set to get the first number of the next set (the fourth number). Repeat starting with the fourth number.
15.	E	19	Pattern in the number added - 5, -3, 4, 5, -3, 4. Add 5 to the first number to get the second. Add -3 to (subtract 3 from) the second number to get the third. Add 4 to the third number to get the fourth. Repeat follow the pattern of the number added.
16.	D	12	Sets of 3 - Multiply the first number in the set by 2 to get the second number in the set then multiply the first number in the set by 3 to get the third. Subtract 3 from the first number in the set to get the first number of the next set (the fourth number). Repeat starting with the fourth number.
17.	C	8	Multiply the first number by 2 to get the second number, divide the second number by 3 to get the third. Repeat starting with the third number.

18. C 29 Set of 3, Add 3 Add 5; Add 12 to the fist number in the first set to get the first number in the second set (repeat)
Sets of 3 – Add 3 to the first number to get the second and add 5 to the second number to get the third (completing the first set of 3). Then add 12 to the first number in first set to get the first number of the next set (the fourth number). Repeat starting with the fourth number.

Figure Matrices

1.	B	Serial Reasoning	The figure is placed in the pattern. The figure is placed in the pattern and the figure is placed in the pattern.
2.	E	Figure Analogy	In the second column a petal is added to one side (shaded). In the third column, a petal is added to the opposite side. While answer A could be correct. The "best" answer is E.
3.	D	Serial Reasoning	Each cell includes a square with a number of circles along the left side of the square. The one circle is placed in the pattern. Two circles are placed in the pattern and three circles are placed in the pattern. The circles are black in the pattern. The circles are gray in the pattern and the circles are white in the pattern.
4.	E	Serial Reasoning	The figure is placed in the pattern. The figure is placed in the pattern and the figure is placed in the pattern.
5.	E	Figure Analogy	In each row, the first two figures are combined - by overlapping - to create the third figure.
6.	C	Serial Reasoning	The figure is placed in the pattern. The figure is placed in the pattern and the figure is placed in the pattern.
7.	D	Serial Reasoning	The figure is placed in the pattern. The figure is placed in the pattern and the figure is placed in the pattern.
8.	C	Figure Analogy	To create the figure in the third column, the figure in the second column is placed over the figure in the first column. While several answers could be correct (whether you choose to believe the white cross is white or simply an outline of a cross,) the "best" answer is C.

9.	A	Serial Reasoning	The figure is placed in the pattern. The figure is placed in the pattern and the figure is placed in the pattern.
10.	B	Figure Analogy	To get the figure in the third column, the figure in the second column is flipped.
11.	C	Serial Reasoning	The figure is placed in the pattern. The figure is placed in the pattern and the figure is placed in the pattern.
12.	E	Figure Analogy	To get the figure in the second column, shade one slice clockwise from the shaded section in the first column. To get the figure in the third column, skip a slice and then shade one slice clockwise from the shaded section in the second column.
13.	C	Figure Analogy	The first two figures in each row are combined to create the third figure.
14.	D	Serial Reasoning	The figure is placed in the pattern. The figure is placed in the pattern and the figure is placed in the pattern.
15.	C	Pattern Completion	The figure is placed in the pattern. The figure is placed in the pattern and the figure is placed in the pattern.
16.	D	Serial Reasoning	The figure is placed in the pattern. The figure is placed in the pattern and the figure is placed in the pattern. An inner horizontal line is placed in the pattern and an inner circle is placed in the pattern. No inner shape is placed in the pattern.
17.	B	Pattern Completion	There are five figures as you go across the rows. Starting with the sixth figure, the five figures are repeated.

18.	D	Pattern Completion	The figures are in pairs going around the outside cells starting with the top left and top middle figures. The pair that includes the missing figure also includes the bottom middle figure.
19.	A	Serial Reasoning	The figure is placed in the pattern . The figure is placed in the pattern and the figure is placed in the pattern . The color is modified in the pattern .
20.	A	Serial Reasoning	The figure is used in the pattern . The figure is used in the pattern and the figure is used in the pattern . A large version of the figure is placed in the pattern . A small version of the figure is placed in the pattern and a combination of the large and small figures is placed in the pattern .
21.	C	Serial Reasoning	The outer figure is placed in the pattern and the outer figure is placed in the pattern . No outer figure is placed in the pattern . No inner figure is placed in the pattern . The figure is placed in the pattern and the figure is placed in the pattern .
22.	D	Figure Analogy	The figures in the second and third columns are combined to create the figure in the first column. Alternatively, the lines in the second column are removed from the figure in the first column to create the third figure.

Paper Folding

1. D
2. B
3. B
4. D
5. A
6. E
7. E
8. C
9. B
10. E
11. E
12. B
13. A
14. D
15. A
16. A

Figure Classification

1. E All figures in the group have a horizontal and vertical line separating the figure into quarters. The top left quarter of the figure is shaded and all four quarters are equal in size.
2. E All figures in the group include one shape ⌈, two shapes ⌋ and two straight lines.
3. E All figures in the group have the same outer shape and two dots. Answers A, C and E fit these criteria. In addition, each section contains only one dot and no dots are on the gray section. The "best" answer is E.
4. C All figures in the group have the same outer/largest shape.
5. A All figures in the group are a rotation of the same figure.
6. D All figures in the group include two lines that are identical. Answers A, B and D fit these criteria. In addition, the lines are not touching and the lines are not straight. The "best" answer is D.
7. C All figures in the group have four shapes that are mirror images across both the horizontal and vertical axis.
8. B All figures in the group have one more line below the horizontal line than above the line.
9. C There is no answer choice that is a clear answer, so the student should pick the "best" answer. The "best" answer has three matching shapes in the square.
10. B Each figure contains a zigzag line and one or more perpendicular lines. All figures in the group have a maximum of one perpendicular line on each line of the zigzag.
11. A All figures in the group have a top shape and a bottom shape that are made from two different shapes. The top shape and the bottom shape reverse the inner and outer shapes.
12. A All figures in the group have the outer triangles facing the same direction (counterclockwise).
13. D All figures in the group are a rotation of the same figure.
14. C All figures in the group have the same four shapes in the matrix cells.

15. B All figures in the group have four shapes in an order of decreasing size. The three larger shapes are the same shape and the smallest is a different shape. Answers A and B fit this criteria. In addition, the shapes are in a clockwise direction from the smallest to the largest, making the answer B.
16. A All figures in the group have an outer and middle shape that is the same shape.
17. C All figures in the group include a circle, a square, a triangle and two dots. Neither dot is in the circle.
18. D All figures in the group reverse the colors of the shapes (outer and center shapes) in the second cell of the figure.
19. C There are two figures – those with white circles and those with gray circles. All figures in the group are a rotation of one of those two figures.
20. A All figures in the group have a bottom branch that starts on the left.
21. A All figures in the group have more dots on the top half of the rectangle/domino than the bottom.
22. A All figures in the group have lines that go from the outside of the white square to the center of the blue circle (behind the circle) and no lines that go from one side of the white square to the other side.

Progress Chart

Follow your progress as you complete the practice test by using the chart below. As you complete each subtest, total the number of correct answers and color in the number in the appropriate column.

When you have completed all of the subtests, use the percentage of correct answers with the information from the Steps to Improve Scores in the next section.

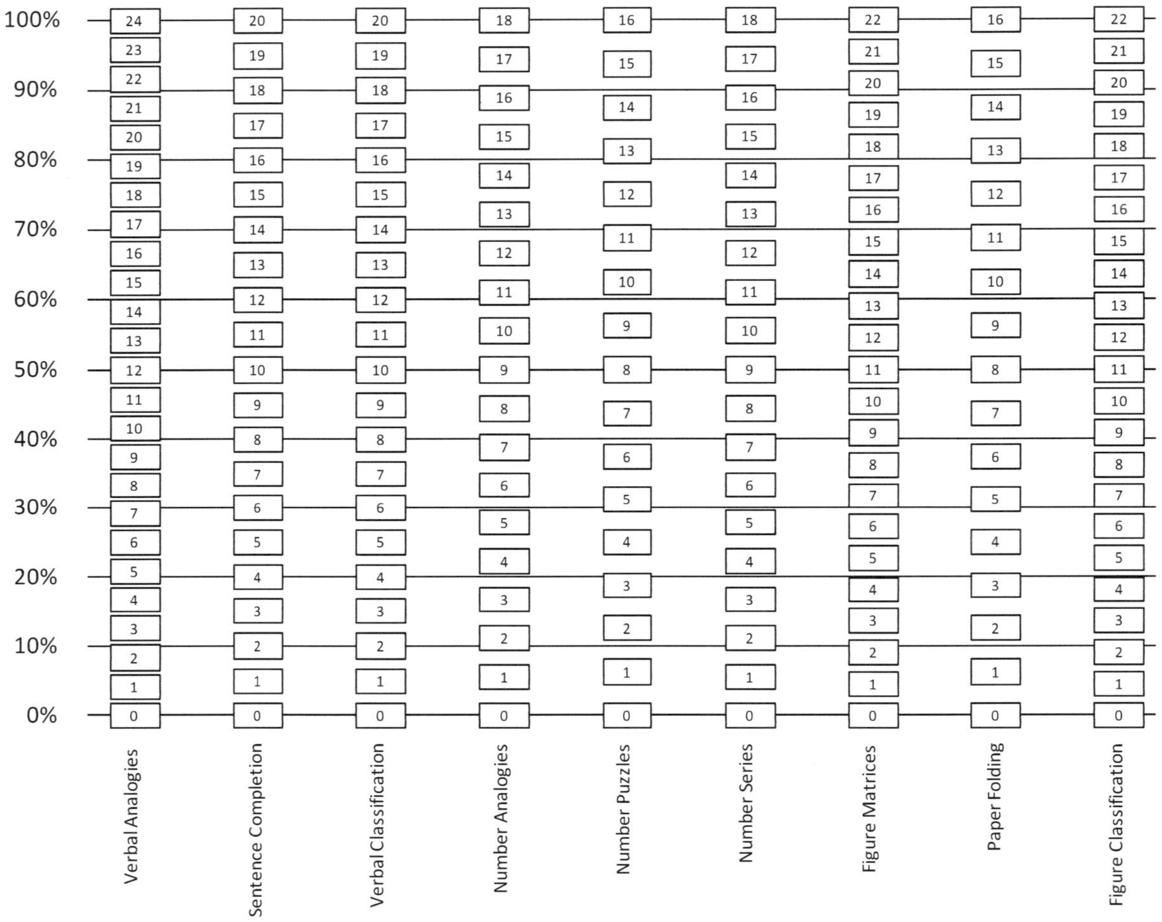

* This practice test has not been standardized with Riverside Publishing and the actual CogAT® exam. Therefore, a valid CogAT® score cannot be concluded from the results on this practice test.

Steps to Improve Scores

Once your child takes one of our practice exams, there are several proactive steps that you can take that may increase your child's score. Depending on the size of the program at your school and the applicant pool, most schools take the top 1 - 5% of applicants. If your child scores below the 90th percentile on the exam, the chances are very low that your child will be eligible for their school's gifted program.

Each child is different, has different skills and abilities, and each child will react differently to tests, practice tests and instruction. Over the years, we have compiled through our own research and feedback from parents, what works.

Step 1 – Review the Practice Test You Completed

If your child answered any questions wrong, have them try those questions again. If your child guessed on any questions, have them try those questions again as well. Reread all the questions and have your child give a reason why they answered the question the way they did. This level of review and understanding will help your child process the concepts of the test area. Like most things, practice and repetition are extremely helpful.

Step 2 – Don't Panic if Your Child Scores Poorly on the First Practice Test.

Most kids have never taken a test like this. The questions and concepts may be foreign to how your child thinks and processes information. You may notice that after the first several questions in a section, your child's success rate starts to improve. Be patient with your child and let them learn what is being asked; their scores will improve with practice. Many parents have reported to us that their child's scores improved by as much as 50% after using our materials.

Step 3 - Additional Practice Questions

If your child received 80% or higher score on our exam, consider pushing them to take a practice test at the next grade level. The other Multilevel Ed. exams have the same types of questions as the questions in this practice test, but the questions become more difficult as they increase in level.

If your child scored under 80% after a couple of attempts at the test, you might consider purchasing Mercer Publishing's How To Guides (See our website at www.mercerpublishing.com). These guides have effective step-by-step instructions as well as additional practice activities for core skills tested on the CogAT®* exam. These guides are designed to increase your child's skills and confidence.

Step 4 – Be Ready, Physically, on Exam Day.

This sound obvious but it surprises us how many times a child is not physically prepared to take the exam. A smart child who is tired or hungry may not score as well as they could on the exam.

- Get a good night's sleep before the exam – preferably 9 or 10 hours. Less sleep means the child will need to use energy reserves to get through the day.
- Eat a healthy breakfast which includes fruit and complex carbohydrates – like whole grain bread or cereal. This balance creates a more constant stream of energy your child will need to stay focused. High sugar cereals, donuts, and sugar drinks will cause your child's blood sugar to fall dramatically during the exam eroding their focus.
- Make sure your child uses the restroom before the exam. Many schools will not allow your child to go to the restroom during the exam. Children who have to go to the restroom and are not allowed to go are distracted from the exam and may not do as well as they could.
- Parents need to be calm and supportive. As a parent, you have done all you can by using these practice tests and tools. You have ensured that your child understands what each subtest is asking and practiced questions with them. Most children understand that this is an important exam, but added pressure from parents will increase their test anxiety.